ON A DARK NIGHT WITH ENOUGH WIND...

To the courageous women
of the countryside
everywhere

ON A DARK NIGHT WITH ENOUGH WIND...

Lilla Pennant

First impression: 2020

Cover design: Sion Ilar
Illustrations: Meyriel Edge & Paul Lloyd
For further information: MyHengiBooks@gmail.com

ISBN: 978 1 78461 827 8

Published and printed in Wales
on paper from well-maintained forests by
Y Lolfa Cyf., Talybont, Ceredigion SY24 5HE
website: www.ylolfa.com
e-mail: ylolfa@ylolfa.com
tel: 01970 832 304
fax: 832 782

Acknowledgements

THIS BOOK IS my retelling of stories from the village called Tremeirchion where I was born in North Wales. Most of these tales are sewn together from intriguing fragments, but four men told me the stories that form a whole chapter or more: Trevor Jones, Bluebell; Dai Lloyd, Cildaugoed; John Rhewys Morris of Mynydd Bychan and Trevor Jones, Bryn Ffynnon. Without them this book could not have been written.

Many other people gave up their blustery winter evenings to talk to me, including Eifion Morris, Phyllis Edwards of Ffynnon Beuno, Margaret Pennant from Henblas Hall, Reverend Bryant, Arthur Pennant of Nantlys, Terry Bryer, the school; Eunice Lloyd Ellis, Reverend Phillip Pennant, Sarah Parry of Rock Cottage, Mair Edwards, Will Williams of Henblas Farm, George Smith of Nant Gwilym, Edward Price, Gerry Crewdson, Mrs Jones, Henafon; Mrs Kennedy, Miss Davies, Mrs Pendleton, who once lived at Nantgwilym Uchaf, David and Alice Pennant, Donald and John Dyke, Lottie Southall, Elwyn Edwards, the post; Cyril Jones, Schoolhouse; Dan Owen of Gwern Hwlkyn, John Evans, Richard Haslam, Rachel Hotham, Banks Hughes of Merllyn, Hannah Humphreys, Lewis Jones, once of Bryn Goleu; Ann Jones (Sain Ffagan Amgueddfa Werin Cymru), Mrs Ridler, Matron of St Clare's Nursing Home; Roger Pendleton, Edward Price, Lloyd Roberts and Fiona Taylor of the Salusbury Arms. Thanks too to the Flintshire Record Office, Charlotte

Evans of the BBC and Eirian Jones of Y Lolfa for helping this project to grow.

The development of these stories owes everything to the encouragement, laughter and wisdom of Christine Lehner, Mary-Ann Tirone Smith, Sarah Clayton, Rebecca Rice, Susan Allport, Juanita Carlson, Babette Kiesel and Eliza Walton. Beside our different firesides this second storytelling slowly took shape.

Last, but not least, my husband Michael Newbold. It is only through his dedication to these stories of the world in which I thought I grew up that this book has finally seen the light of day.

In Tremeirchion people were usually known by just a first name and where they lived. The list above is organized mostly in the order that I met and interviewed people and includes, where possible, the name of the house or farm if they lived or had lived in Tremeirchion or the nearby community of Sodom. Some people were so well known that their first name needed no qualification.

Many names in Tremeirchion were still fluid. Though it was always spoken the same, the house where I lived while I was researching this book could still quite acceptably be spelt three or four different ways, as one, two or three words, depending on my mood.

Since I wrote this book in the 1980s, genetic research has found that the descendants of the earliest surviving race in all of the British Isles were to be found not in Scotland or Ireland, but in North Wales, or the mountainous world of North-West Wales to be precise. This was the birthplace of a family whose unusual way of life is the starting point of this book.

Contents

Foreword

HAVE YOU EVER walked through rough countryside at night? A moonless, stormy, winter's night – with no flashlight to hold that suffocating darkness at bay? You can't even see your feet let alone where you're putting them. And then there's a wind – not light intermittent gusts, but hard, relentless shafts of cold air rattling every branch and leafless twig. You're surrounded by an orchestra of wood percussionists and wind whistlers.

On those impossible winter nights, the men from nearly every family in the Welsh countryside where I grew up were hard at work. Some of them, loving the absurdity and challenge of it all; others working quietly, hoping to come away with enough money to feed their family for a few weeks until the next dark, stormy, winter's night.

How did they see? They didn't – they couldn't. But each man learned to see without seeing, just as a blind man does, and could move as swiftly at night as he did by day. To find the way, each man had to know where things should be, to hear where a wood ended by the sound of the grass ahead. Some trees sounded different – the big oaks firm, but their hundreds of small branches thrashing wildly in the wind high up; the elms and ashes not so sturdy, creaking as whole trees bent in the wind. They got to know the sounds under their feet, the feel of mud and grass, paths and leaves. They learned to read the signs of what was closest, and follow lines in the landscape – a hedge they could feel at arm's length, a fence the wind whistled through, a stream that bubbled and splashed.

But even after fifty years of going into that strange primordial chaos, even for the most skilful, the canniest old-timer, there were no guarantees. Everyone took a chance on nights like these. There was no way to be safe, no way to be sure that the men they had to avoid were not waiting behind this tree or that stile. The man who stood still was the safest, but the hunters had to move fast and far to catch anything at all. And at any point on their journey their nemesis might be waiting quietly behind a wall or gate.

Strangely enough, many of these men began to feel safest when they were closest to the house where I grew up, where logically they had the most to fear. My family owned more land than anyone else in the area. They were the main employer and owned most of the houses in which these men lived. They had the power to instantly dispossess.

The skill of those night-time hunters made them look down on people who only worked by day, seeing them as lacking in the real arts of the countryside. The men who worked at night became their own elite, and they guarded the secrets of their society with as much skill as they navigated the darkness.

As a child all I knew was that there was something going on that I didn't know about. The veil of secrecy over what happened at night, which was absolute in the presence of older members of my family, had not been so complete when I was very young. Maybe the people who worked in my home by day thought a small child wouldn't understand or remember. I didn't know what people were hiding, but I grew up feeling sure there was a secret, and secrets fascinated me.

Why were these cheerful people with all their rural wit and wisdom hiding something? How bad could it be? I decided early on that it wasn't bad – it was just that no one wanted to tell us, the people from the Hall. But as I grew older, these mysterious hints disappeared. That really puzzled me. The wiser I should have been, the less I seemed to know or understand of the wild countryside around me and the people who lived there.

At the age of twenty-six, after living away from Wales for eight years, I came back to try as an adult to get to know the village where I had grown up. Instead of waiting for people to talk, I moved into an abandoned house on the hill. There was no power or heating, except for two wood fires and a small wood stove, and the only way to get there was a footpath through the wood.

I went out and started to ask questions. Everyone was surprised. By tradition my family and the people who lived around us kept apart, except for the usual day-to-day business and celebrations. We spoke only English. They preferred Welsh. Why was I asking questions? The men who had the most to tell closed ranks around the secret I was approaching too closely. They set out to distract me and entertain me with a host of other funny and sad stories about 'the characters' who had lived in the village. They almost succeeded.

1

On the mountain

EVEN AS A young child, I sensed that I was surrounded by a mystery that involved me – or rather my family – but that was more connected with the hills that rose up a quarter of a mile from my home. This steep ridge had always been called 'the mountain' by locals – something that used to make our English visitors laugh. The highest summit in the area barely reaches seven hundred feet above sea level. A mountain is something different, these travellers would explain, it had to be at least a thousand feet high. I wasn't convinced.

To me, a hill was something you could climb up and down in an afternoon's stroll, just a minor interruption on a rolling plain. This high ground was something different. When you travelled up there, you moved into a different world. But I was never able to explain why.

The high ground in this region sometimes erupts into the craggy peaks for which Wales is famous, but for the most part consists of huge rolling plateaus and rounded hills, all that remains of high mountains long ago. The tops of these plateaus used to be covered with purple-flowering heather, while the slopes and tiny stream valleys were crowded with bracken which unfurled poisonous emerald fronds in spring. Throughout the summer the bracken pushed up and out until it had formed a solid dark-green mass as high and higher than a man. In winter it reverted to a maze of soft purplish-brown stalks which bristled and crackled when an animal pushed through.

Less neglected pastures sported clumps of gorse, a fiercely spiked shrub, whose yellow flowers spread a lemony sweetness across the hillsides on sunny spring days. Nowhere were the people of North Wales more conservative than in these hills.

Until the 1980s the only inhabitants up there lived in small farmhouses or long, low cottages built of local stone. These isolated cottage dwellers and farmers didn't seem to be interested in money or progress, only in continuing their own special eccentric way of life. I often wondered what different clock operated up there that made these people resist the modern ways of the towns and valleys. I knew that it wasn't a lack of money that had held one particular family back. This family, the most stubbornly traditional of all, lived on a farm which showed barely any trace of the twentieth century, and not much of the nineteenth, either.

The house and farm lay landlocked in a small private valley between two hill summits. There was no road, not even a recognisable cart track up to or anywhere near the house. How could there be? Lizzie, and her brother Richard Hugh, the sole occupants since their parents died, rarely left their farm and, if they did, they travelled on foot. I visited Lizzie when I was a child and was instantly drawn to her. She was a tiny woman, not short or stocky, but well proportioned and graceful. Her size became her. With her deeply-wrinkled smiling face, she reminded me of the pictures in children's fairy tales of tiny people, but she couldn't walk in a straight line; she walked in a slow-moving 'S' hook. I was told later this was the result of a lifetime of carrying water up from the spring in the yard below.

More than anyone else on 'the mountain', she welcomed my family into her old-fashioned kitchen. Unlike her neighbours she didn't seem to be at all inhibited. While she was directing each of us to her old, hard-bottomed chairs, she would enquire, 'Would you like a cup of tea?'

Welsh was Lizzie's first language, but with her head curled over somewhat towards the floor, her English flowed without any hint of Welsh. My mother was always tempted to accept the tea, but she only agreed once, and Lizzie prepared such a strong dark brew that my mother declined from then on. It became just a ritual, and the steaming old black kettle on the hob by the fire was undisturbed.

Lizzie would settle back in her old armchair and ask about our lives. She seemed so much in control. People visited as if they were doing her a favour, but left having done no more than unburden themselves to this reclusive old woman. She never talked about her own life. To us she never complained, never boasted, never even described what had happened to her – and yet she seemed to be more canny and alert than anyone else I knew in Tremeirchion.

Lizzie loved the peace of life on the hilltops. After her brother died in 1972, the vicar of Tremeirchion pressed her to move down to the valley so she wouldn't be so isolated.

'Dim o gwbl. Allen ni'm neud â phobl yn busnesa trwy'r amser.' ['Oh no,' she replied quickly. 'I couldn't be doing with people poking their noses in all the time.']

Even the people who had given up trying to understand Lizzie were intrigued by the interior of her house, which had changed only in small details since around 1700 when most of the oak furniture in the house was made. Near the end of her life Lizzie still sat by the fire in a chair with the date 1646 worked into the ornately carved high back. It was as if the clock had stopped here around that time, but I always had the feeling that things had not stood still on the mountain, that something had happened, which made these and other hill dwellers cling on to their secluded life.

I grew up at the other end of this village, just two miles away but in a different landscape in the protected valley.

14

My parents lived in a towering country house built by my great-grandfather in the 1860s. Local people referred to our house simply as 'the Hall'. In a different way from Lizzie and Richard Hugh, our family had also remained close to its past. We were probably the last family in the whole valley to remain in one of these huge buildings created during the optimism of the mid-nineteenth century. All the other sprawling mansions had been pulled down or turned into private boarding schools – very private, because these houses were built down long drives, deep into the countryside. We had no close neighbours, and I wasn't allowed to play with children of my age in the area.

Our most constant companions were the people who worked for my parents, the women who came to clean and cook each day, the elderly gardeners, 'the men' who worked on my father's farm, and one teenage boy, John Lidford, who came on some soft and sunny summer afternoons to ride with my sister and me on our ponies.

All year round my sister and I spent most of our spare time tending to and riding our small sure-footed ponies but, when we rode, we almost never rode into the valley which surrounded us on three sides. There it lay, an endless series of gates to open into one muddy field after another, corn crops to skirt around, and hungry herds of bullocks who pounded over to encircle us on our smaller ponies.

Instead, we took to the hills where we could ride for miles up old bridle paths, ancient drover routes, and even earlier pathways that had never been paved. Some of the hilltop fields stretched for more than a quarter of a mile, full of curious hollows, copses in the bottoms of tiny valleys, open moorland and thin winding sheep paths. When we galloped over the open ground, the thin soil reverberated against the rock beneath so that at every hoofbeat we could hear a soft thunder.

But the hills were not just open land – in this area there were the remains of ancient cottages long since abandoned, and a whole string of other cottages that had been abandoned only a few years before. In summer you could still find berries, currants and peaches in one of the gardens. At another there were books and letters and old medicine bottles left there by the last occupant.

For the first few years when we rode over the mountain we were accompanied by John, who lived on the hillslopes and who knew all the old tracks and bridle paths. Though he had grown up here, John was different in every way from the short, wiry farmers we met, who would nod so slowly and deliberately that you barely caught a glimpse of their eyes. Unlike most Welsh people, John was fair haired. He was tall – even willowy – and full of talk, jokes and fears. He was never quiet; one minute he'd be bursting with enthusiasm, the next reeling with laughter or scared out of his wits. He was terrified of ghosts and thunderstorms. His father had died digging a ditch in a thunderstorm when it collapsed on him.

It was John who first made me curious about the abandoned houses. He allowed us to stop and explore the tiny stone-built cottages, but he would never tell us about the people who had lived there. If we asked, he would smile and then burst out laughing, but he wouldn't say why. His laughter was rich with some secret joke. At one small, single-storey cottage called Bryn Caredig – that was still occupied by his aunt – he could never help but giggle. It worked on my childish imagination.

At the age of eighteen I left my school in Wales and went to university, first in England and then in America. Coming back to Wales on holidays, I wondered again at the old whispered hints and half-tales that I had heard as a young child in my old home built far from any public road. But my family was living in more isolation than ever, the teams of women who used to tell stories in the kitchen, the elderly gardeners and John had all gone. Only one woman, the retired post lady, herself a storehouse of gossip gathered on her walking postal rounds, still came to the house to help my mother, but without others to talk to she would tell me little. It seemed that if there really was a story behind it all, I would never know.

After I left university I lived in London, then New York. The more I saw of the rest of the world, the more curious the world I grew up in became. Things were changing even there. My father had started to sell the houses he owned on the hilltop. Instead of just falling down, these houses were fetching high prices as sites for people from the towns to build in scenic Wales. One after another the old houses were disappearing. I asked my father to let me renovate what was probably the prettiest house of all on the slopes. He agreed.

I started to work on this house with a group of college friends, which turned into a long procession of visitors from England and America. New friends, actors, set designers and writers would come to Wales for a few days, admire and enthuse, eat and drink, and then leave again. Little work on the house got done. I began to get to know my neighbours and the builders who worked on the house, but even they arrived more often to discuss what was to be done, what might be done and what had been done long ago.

One elderly builder was aptly known as 'Trevor Jones, Bluebell'. There was a lightness, a brightness about this diminutive builder who couldn't have been much over five feet tall. He came to my house for over a year to tell me why he would not be coming the next week to save my barn with its gaping holes and old oak beams, soggy and soft from years of exposure to frequent rain showers. The work did not progress for a year and a half. In the meantime, Trevor Bluebell taught me patience, how to bide my time, and about the resilience of the old country buildings. He started to tell me the stories about this area.

Trevor had a birthmark larger than any I had ever seen. It ran all the way from his forehead to his chin, but his elfin-like love of a good story made it vanish from the thoughts of the onlooker.

A. Carvell

Trevor Jones with me in his garden at Bluebell.

He soon became a friend. We discovered a common curiosity about the old days. His eyes would twinkle as he started to talk, but there seemed to be a great deal more that he might say, if only... If only, what? If only I wasn't the girl from the Hall? My family had lived there for four generations, and my father could trace his ancestry back to some of the ancient princes of Wales.

In truth I was neither fully English, nor fully Welsh. By inclination I was Welsh, but I knew I was an outsider in the world where I had grown up. Trevor Jones, Bluebell, never told me the stories I saw twinkling behind his dark, bright eyes, but I sensed an invitation. The world was changing. Even a girl from the big house might tumble into this rich kingdom, if only she could find the way.

2

Lizzie

IN 1976 THE most traditional and most mysterious farm in this area fell empty. Lizzie, the last of her family, had died. She had no children, not even a nephew or niece. Following traditional Welsh land rights, she and her brother had equal claim on the farm; if one married, normally that person would have to leave. Lizzie and Richard Hugh chose to stay on and never marry. According to her will, her savings were to be divided between a small group of friends that included my father, and the rest of her possessions were to be sold for charity.

At the time I didn't question how odd it was for someone living in a remote two-up, two-down house to make my father, the owner of a big house in the valley, her executor and one of the main beneficiaries of her will. Lizzie's family and my family had always been close. I didn't think to ask why. My father wasn't cut from standard cloth; he was Lizzie's landlord, but he seemed to be more her friend, and vice versa.

Normally, when there is no close family, the job of clearing the house is taken on by a junk or antique dealer for a lump sum depending on the quality of the contents. I knew that if this household was sold outright, anything without immediate cash value would be burnt on the spot or carted away as rubbish. So I asked if I could take on the task of clearing out Penuchaf.

From the fields around the house you could see far across the valley below and, on fine days, all the way to the peaks of Snowdonia fifty miles away. Everything up here was sparse. The outlines of the land stood out clearly under a thin mantle of grass and small stunted trees. The farm buildings were tucked into the side of a rocky outcrop around a spring which bubbled up in the yard, providing the only water supply for the farm.

I loved the wild simplicity of this landscape. I felt free up here in a way I never felt in the valley or at the house where I grew up. And so it was, with a sense of privilege, that one fine May day I drove across the tight turf of the open field to the house. I was full of curiosity and strange fears. There was something about Penuchaf and Lizzie that was odd and disturbing. Even Lizzie's best friends in the village said they wouldn't dare as much as pass through Penuchaf farmyard at night, now that she had gone. Lizzie and her brother Richard Hugh were different from everybody else. Thirty years before, when most of the other hilltop houses were occupied, they wouldn't have been so noticeable. But after everyone else had left, how did they survive such isolation, physically and mentally, and why?

The hills around here are full of history and strange stories. It's not just a romantic idea based on their bleak grandeur – these hills were the main centre of life for the first people who lived in Wales. These nomadic hunters camped out on the hillslopes because the valleys were forested swamps, impenetrable and threatening because of the sabre-toothed tigers and wolves that lurked there. Some of the earliest man-made flint tools found in Wales were discovered in 1886 in the caves of the little valley carved out by the spring that rises at Penuchaf.

For thousands of years these early peoples stayed on the hilltops and buried their dead there in mounds or tumuli – there are nearly a dozen in the vicinity of Penuchaf – the nearest, a huge cairn with one side like a face peering out from beneath a

A. Carvell

Penuchaf (the upper head) sits by itself in a saucer-like depression between two summits. The old road up to the house was completely disused. The only way to get there was across one or the other of two huge fields.

shawl, stands just behind the house. It is so large that it is now considered to be just a freak of nature. Another much smaller earth mound a few fields away was excavated around 1870 but, on the second day working there, the labourers employed to dig the mound fled and refused to return. These ancient remains were long respected and feared for the curses they were believed to carry against grave robbers.

Traces of ancient religions linger in the hills. A few summits to the south is Moel Famau, a smooth heather-clad mound whose name, 'the hill of the Mothers', goes back to the earliest known religion in Wales, a worship of mother gods believed to reside on certain mountaintops.

I felt something like a grave robber too, crossing the field to Penuchaf to empty the house of this intensely private family, and even worse to investigate into the affairs of the mysterious Lizzie, or Miss Jones as she was always referred to in my family. I started the task, assuring myself it would only take a few mornings and afternoons. I would be finished and away within a week. Then I would know for certain, one way or another, about Penuchaf and the people of the hilltops. I was wrong in almost every way.

The old door was stiff. With no fire glowing in the grate to keep it dry, the wood had expanded in the damp spring weather. As the door scraped back over the big slate slabs, I found the kitchen just as I remembered it: the oak rack still full of clean blue-and-white plates, the chairs by the fire ready to receive guests and the Victorian cooking grate only needing paper, wood and a little bit of coal to start to warm the kettle again. Everything was in order until I looked inside the old oak furniture and found that Lizzie and Richard Hugh seemed to have kept everything that arrived at Penuchaf in their lifetime, and everything they had inherited from their parents and family before.

Drawers, cupboards, tiny portable wooden desks, Bible boxes, old tin tea caddies and blanket chests were all stuffed to the top – and a bit more – with papers, clothes, rags, old razor knives and ancient cutlery. And yet the house was not a mess. Until her last illness Lizzie kept Penuchaf gleaming. She told her regular visitors not to come on a Tuesday because that was the day she cleaned and polished the old cast-iron cooking grate and all of its dozen or more cast-iron implements, including a complicated crane to hold a kettle over the firebox. The same day she took all the plates and ornaments off the high old-fashioned oak dresser and polished each one and the whole dresser before putting them back. There was almost nothing in the room that belonged to the twentieth century.

This little front room was all that visitors ever saw, but we all wondered, with this collection of antiques occupying the main living room of the house, what lurked in the other less-used rooms of the house – the parlour for instance, a shadowy room at the best of times? Parlours were only used in Wales for large formal gatherings, weddings and funerals. Lizzie and

Meyriel Edge

The open fire, on which Lizzie cooked all of her meals and brewed the tea she offered to us when we called.

Richard Hugh had never used the parlour except for the annual harvest and threshing suppers, when they entertained all their neighbours and friends who had helped them that day.

The parlour at Penuchaf was dominated by a large gateleg table and eight high-backed dining chairs. Two big oak chests stood along one wall on either side of the fireplace, with the dates and initials of marriages in 1642 and 1684 carved into the central panel. In the next generation, this family had acquired a tall cupboard, also with the date of the marriage, 1711, carved into the board at the top. But the most interesting piece of furniture, a huge old *cwpwrdd tridarn* (three-layered cupboard), had no date.

This uniquely Welsh piece of furniture had large cupboards below a line of drawers followed by a second row of smaller cupboards topped by an open section covered with a wooden canopy. In the days when *tridarns* were first made, a family could store most of their possessions in this one piece of furniture. The Penuchaf *tridarn* possessed an extra layer of drawers, as well as some fine ball-shaped finials hanging down from the upper section, making it an unusually fine *tridarn*, one of the best of its type. The old *tridarn* was even finer than it seemed.

Before Lizzie died the only thing she told my father about the contents of the house was that there was gold in a drawer in the big old *tridarn*. The six drawers contained nothing but old tablecloths and a few silver spoons. We went over the cupboard carefully. There was no other drawer, but there was one blocked panel with no way in. No part of the panel moved, and there was no small lever or button that we could find. An optimist, even in defeat, my father said there probably wasn't anything in there anyway. I went back to sorting out the other drawers and cupboards.

In the other drawers, cupboards, tins, boxes and desks there was a deluge of old and new papers: village circulars announcing special celebrations in the village all the way back to Queen Victoria's Diamond Jubilee, farming bills and receipts, general household goods, even food receipts, Christmas cards and letters, accounts and diaries. They were all there. Many of the older bills were beautifully written out, describing exactly what work was done, which horse had been shod. Some bills even invited debtors to a big annual dinner where their bills could be settled. As the papers became more recent, so did the numbers of official government forms and receipts.

I could see the evidence of Lizzie and Richard Hugh's day-to-day life, from the certificates for their achievements in school to the accounts of this small farm and Lizzie's contribution in milking the cows, making butter and tending the hens.

In the little back kitchen there was a broad, sturdy bench for slaughtering a pig each spring and autumn, and a table covered with large flat earthenware 'crocks' in which the new milk was set after each milking so that the cream could rise quickly and easily to the top. The next day it would be skimmed and stored in jars until there was enough to churn into butter. This luxurious butter wasn't eaten at home. It all went to market in Denbigh each Wednesday.

I even found the basket hanging on the back of the door in the tiny larder in which the butter and eggs were taken to market. I noticed it, but didn't realize its significance. It had two quite separate compartments, a deep lower compartment closed off by the two-hinged basketwork flaps that formed the upper compartment. It would be impossible to get into the lower compartment without emptying the contents of the upper compartment first. What seemed an inconvenient design, I discovered years later, was entirely deliberate. This market basket was well known in the neighbourhood.

There were, in fact, a host of different hiding places around this little house. I discovered most of them by accident: false bottoms to drawers in blanket chests, a little bedside table with a secret compartment ingeniously concealed in the back panel. I discovered this hiding place and others because I had to prepare each piece of furniture for sale and, as I tipped up drawers and picked up pieces of furniture, the secret panels moved or slid out. They were completely empty.

The steep wooden stairs opened into one bedroom with a big double bed, which Lizzie's parents must once have occupied. This room would be kept warm summer and winter

Upstairs were
two simple
bedrooms,
with one
leading out of
the other.

Meyriel Edge

from the fire below. The Edwardian iron bedstead had a quilt made from many strips of old dresses – simple cotton fabrics that had been well used before being reused for a spread that had since been patched and patched again. The second room had two wide brass and iron twin beds – one covered with another quilt made of simple cottons. In the corner stood a walnut chest of drawers from the time of Queen Anne. The elaborate barley-twist legs and stretchers had long since worn away and were now reduced to one stub. Richard Hugh had fixed up the rest with a construction of red bricks.

There was no outer staircase to the back bedroom, which are still sometimes to be found in very old Welsh farmhouses. It was a side entrance that allowed the eldest unmarried daughter to receive young male suitors and avoid wasting coal on the fire if her visitor stayed too long. The current farmhouse at Penuchaf was too recent; the Methodist and Baptist congregations all over Wales had disapproved and had put an end to 'bundling' long before it was built.

When all of the furniture had been cleared, I invited some of the leading dealers in oak furniture to come to the house to buy. The first dealer to arrive was canny to the tricks of the makers of the *tridarns*. In less than a minute he had pushed a series of well-disguised blocks behind the panel to release the centre panel. It swung open to reveal not only a large inner space but a set of tiny drawers each receding into a smaller upper one, like a set of steps. They were beautifully made and so well crafted that they showed no signs of age. This secret set of drawers held the oldest documents in the house.

There were the wills of the Hughes' of Cae Gwyn going back to the 1600s, from whom Lizzie and Richard Hugh had ultimately inherited this houseful of furniture; the Bill of Sale when Penuchaf had been purchased by my great-grandfather in 1866, and an old diary from the 1700s with scribbled calculations of the flock in a language special to shepherds, most of which is no longer known; and finally three golden guineas. The gold was enclosed in a letter from Richard Hugh as a soldier in the First World War. It was his pay. He wrote, 'there's not much use having these jingling around in my pocket,' and so he sent them home. And they, like him, never thought of spending them.

There was a rumour in the village that Lizzie and Richard Hugh had kept a lot of money hidden in one of the old straw mattresses. A month or so after Lizzie died, a burglar broke in and took most of the Victorian ornaments, some of the old jet jewellery and a couple of fob watches, at the same time as slashing each mattress looking for the money. But the Jones' were no fools. They had long since stopped storing their money in the house as people used to do in country cottages, often hiding their money in compartments above the fire which could only be reached when the fire was good and cold.

The central panel of the *cwpwrdd tridarn* opened at last to reveal a set of beautifully made tiny drawers.

Meyriel Edge

I kept all these papers – even the bank statements – because I couldn't make head nor tail of it all. There was something missing. It never dawned on me that there might be a secret which was so difficult that the Jones' would conceal it even in the privacy of their own home and in letters to their closest friends.

Late one afternoon, as the light was beginning to fade, I was hurrying to empty one of the drawers of the kitchen dresser so that I could be out of Penuchaf before dark. The drawer was entirely full of tightly-tied rag bundles. Could these bundles so carefully tied be just rags – just a store of fabrics for future patches? Some of the blouses that I had found upstairs contained a patch on patch so that it was almost impossible to find the original blouse.

As I started to open the bundles, a large shadow fell over me from the open doorway a few feet away. In that instant I thought of the isolation of Penuchaf – no phone, no road, no one close by. I looked up and saw the outline of a lean, wiry man with curly dark hair. He stared down at me and at the bundles of rags. He didn't speak. I clambered to my feet, the tightly-tied bundles falling to the floor all around. The strange man was young, probably only a few years older than me. He had dark, quiet eyes which contrasted with his very pale complexion.

'Hello,' he half mumbled. His lack of ease did nothing to reassure me. I feebly repeated his greeting. He seemed almost proprietorial about this house, as though I was fiddling with things that belonged to him. He was right – in a way.

When he finally overcame what turned out to be a deep shyness and surprise at finding me here, alone, he mentioned his name, and I realized that he was joint executor with my father. He was a hill farmer and Lizzie's nearest neighbour at the time she died. I felt awkward – here I was, handling the contents of her house, with its valuable old furniture, by arrangement with my father, but without ever meeting or being introduced to the other executor whose decisions should have ranked with my father's.

But Eifion was a quiet man. He wanted to see what I was doing, and when he had, he seemed satisfied, though sad and mystified like everyone else to see the dispersal of this curious ancient household. Lizzie's will was a puzzle to both her executors. Why had her will made no mention of the beautiful old furniture she had looked after so well?

But more than anything Eifion Morris seemed puzzled why I should have taken on the task of clearing this now damp and musty farm. I tried to explain. I told him about the papers at Penuchaf and that I had always wanted to find out more about the Jones' and the old hill dwellers.

'Not much to say is there?' he said, using the Welsh habit of turning a sentence around at the end to make it into a question that doesn't expect a reply. He had a point. It all depended on whether people like him could tell me something more.

'Oh yes,' I said, looking for a tactful way. 'There is something about these hills, you know, this area just around here. I would like to write about it. The Jones' were the last family... I would love to know more about them. Do you know...'

He looked away at the room and said softly, 'It's my father you'd have to talk to. He's the one that knows.' He looked more puzzled and doubtful than before and swung out of the doorway and away without another word.

In the following few weeks more antique dealers came and went, each one taking another load away from Penuchaf. The highest price went for the old *tridarn*, with its secret row of drawers behind the centre panel. It went directly to the National Museum of History at St Fagans in South Wales. I travelled to and fro, taking some of the smaller things and china directly to shops in Wales and London. In the end I rented a stall in Portobello Road one Saturday to sell all the little things I had failed to sell elsewhere – right down to cups without a saucer. I sold nearly every piece.

Penuchaf was empty, but for one ornate Edwardian dresser, the only piece of twentieth-century furniture in the house. The price I was offered for it was considered too low by my father and so it remained for a few months before a curious passerby took it themselves.

I travelled down to London and back with my boxes of papers and books and my unsolved puzzle. I had so much material on the day-to-day life of the village and only a small, lingering suspicion that something was still missing.

That Christmas I went up to see Eifion and his father. I went just to call in. In rural Wales using the phone was not the courteous way to contact someone. Instead, you went and called, as in the days before the phone came. I was intending just to say hello and ask if old Mr Morris would indeed care to talk to me some other time about the old days, and Lizzie and Richard Hugh. Eifion and his father were in the kitchen, sitting on large soft armchairs in front of the coal fire. Theirs was a spacious country kitchen which had not been modernized and still boasted a traditional scrubbed pine table; however, everything centred around the small coal fire to one side.

Eifion was surprised and just as shy as before. It seemed odd to me, and probably to him too, that we were so close in age and had grown up in the same small village but had never seen each other before we met at Penuchaf. I liked him for his quietness and directness, and most of all the absence of the old polite formality which so often created an impenetrable barrier between my family and our close neighbours. He invited me to sit by the fire. This was not to be a quick formal visit by the door.

As soon as I saw Eifion's father, I realized that good looks ran in the family. John Rhewys Morris' eyes glistened in anticipation. He didn't say anything to start with, but as Eifion talked, he watched me, studying my expressions, then looking away every so often as if chiding himself for his own curiosity. And so Eifion and I had to keep talking but, just as before, Eifion was not an easy person to hold in conversation; he was unable to make small talk and it seemed too soon to ask anything really important – it was easy for the conversation to die.

Soon enough we exhausted the two obvious topics – Lizzie and Richard Hugh, and the fate of Penuchaf. Eifion repeated some of my questions and comments to his father, who mumbled, muttered and smiled, but remained strictly unintelligible. Then Eifion seemed to take pity on me – he spoke to his father again, this time in Welsh.

It was as if a small cog that had been jamming a large mechanism came loose. His father started to talk fluently about Lizzie and Richard Hugh, about neither of them getting married. It amazed the old man that these two had never apparently even wanted to get married. He and Eifion talked about their best memory of Penuchaf – the elaborate harvest teas which Lizzie had provided 'just like they used to be long ago'. He talked about the strange way that Lizzie and Richard Hugh never wanted to go anywhere away from Penuchaf, except to church on Sunday and market every Wednesday where they sold their produce.

Richard Hugh had used a pony and trap with a net thrown over the top to take his sheep to market, and that reminded John Rhewys of the blacksmiths in Tremeirchion, Tom and Jo 'y go'. He started to laugh – this pair of blacksmiths had been so famous for their jokes that even the very serious vicar had been obliged to take some visiting clergymen to meet them. John Rhewys laughed until the tears began to well up in his eyes as he thought of Tom. I couldn't help laughing too.

Through his tears he beamed at me. For the next two hours John Rhewys forgot about Lizzie and Richard Hugh. He told me a story of his own, about the challenge and adventure of finding a wife in Wales in the 1920s.

3

In pursuit of a wife

MYNYDD BYCHAN CANNOT be seen from the road and only people who knew John Rhewys and his son would think to look for a house at the end of the gated track that cut off the ancient road over the summit. There was indeed a tiny sign marked Mynydd Bychan, once black and white, much splashed with mud, but it was so small that no passing motorist could have been expected to see the sign, let alone read it.

The track to the farm curved around the open hillside into this tiny, private valley. Looking west as you approached the house, you could see clearly across the main valley to the moors which extended for more than a dozen miles beyond and, in good weather, you could see as far as the Great Orme's Head jutting out into the sea. This glinting line of blue light, visible at the edge of the horizon, was the open water known as Liverpool Bay on the maps, though no Welsh person gave an English name to this inlet of the Atlantic bordered by the three very different countries of England, Ireland and Wales.

When I approached Mynydd Bychan for the first time, I was elated by this new view of the hillslopes and the valley, and by my impending meeting. Most of the hills and mountains of Wales were smoothed and rounded by the glaciers of the Ice Ages which gouged and crushed the land beneath them. But,

Meyriel Edge

Rock Chapel, which seats less than ten, was built by the neighbouring community of St Beuno and is still used as a place of quiet prayer.

just below Mynydd Bychan stands a rocky pinnacle crowned by a tiny chapel just large enough to hold eight people. The chapel belongs to a Roman Catholic seminary which lies on the secluded slopes below. John Rhewys worked for the home farm of this seminary from the early 1920s until the Depression.

In spite of his eighty-odd years, John Rhewys was tall for a Welshman of his generation, at about five foot ten, but it was in his face that he was most distinct. He had the fine lean features and wide prominent brow that would have suited a statue of a Roman soldier or statesman.

His eyes, though sunken with age, were still quick and bright, and when he smiled his otherwise dignified face folded so deeply that his mouth and eyes almost joined in a beam that was as impish as it was irresistible.

In his thoughts he often glimpsed beyond the straitened circumstances of his own life and yet, unlike his neighbours, he showed no sadness. It was not that he did not remember the limitations, but that they never overwhelmed his keen enjoyment of life.

As a young man John Rhewys hadn't been able to find any work in Tremeirchion that paid him a living wage, and so he had to leave Wales and move to Liverpool, the nearest large industrial area about fifty miles away. Liverpool was no border town, however; it was wholly English, a port with heavy industry and many areas of terraced housing built during the Industrial Revolution. It was also the port from which many Welsh families embarked for America.

'I worked there in building for two years,' he said adding, almost under his breath, 'Labouring, but my father got sick so I came home. I got a job down at the seminary farm. There were six of us then and a shepherd. Mr Wynn was the bailiff – he was strict. I was the teamsman in charge of the horses. Started at six every morning – whatever the weather. I had to be there by the field with all the halters. You couldn't even be a couple of minutes late. In the winter I'd be just standing there in the cold, waiting until it was light enough to see where the horses were.'

He chuckled to himself, 'I stayed there ten years. After the First World War the unions had come in and things began to change, but only a little on the farms.'

John Rhewys did not dwell on his long working hours, but they had been a source of preoccupation for another reason – they seriously affected his pursuit of a wife.

Most of the girls and unmarried women of the village went 'into service', which meant working and living in one of the 'big houses' in the village. There were half a dozen of these, and a few wealthy farmers who could afford one or two 'live-in' servants. The pay, however, was very low, a few shillings a week, and the work went from dawn till dusk on all but one day a week. One woman from Tremeirchion, who was guarded in all she told me, explained bitterly, 'We got half a day a week off, but you were expected to go and see your family then. It took most of my time getting there and back.'

They were also allowed time to go to church or chapel on Sundays. These services became important meeting places each week. The boys and young men of the village would gather together before and after the services, watching and waiting for the neatly dressed girls who would hurry shyly past them. Only the fearless and the desperately-in-love dared to stop a girl with so many others looking on. If a girl was stopped at all, it was usually just a message carried on behalf of another man.

The only other chance to see and be seen was at local weddings. John Rhewys explained, 'At Cae Gwyn, they'd get all dressed up in the morning if they heard there was a wedding that day. They'd be doing the cleaning in their best clothes because Mrs Morgan might come down the passage and call outside the kitchen door, "There's a wedding at the church this afternoon. If anyone wants to go down for an hour, they have permission." Of course, they knew already. They'd be out of the back door in a minute.

'There were a lot of servants in the big houses then, locked in in the evening and let out in the morning. I know, I saw it myself from where I was hiding by the back door. Mr Morgan of Cae Gwyn, he locked the back door himself – sunset in the summer and at five in the winter. It wasn't easy to get up there before the door was locked.

'At Tŷ Mawr the farmer there put barbed wire around the top rail of his gate and then padlocked it. When he came in the morning, he found all sorts of pieces of trousers caught on the spikes.

'But, I knew Cae Gwyn best. I went there when Ivor from the smithy was looking for a wife.'

John Rhewys leaned back against the worn headrest of his armchair. He was grinning to himself, but keeping his eyes on me. He was trying to decide whether to say any more, considering who I was – the daughter of the owner of the largest house in the area. Then something changed inside him.

'We had a few close shaves,' he continued cautiously. 'You see, there's a big bank at the back of the house, at least twenty yards long and nearly as high as a man. You could look over it, but it wasn't easy to climb over, not in a hurry. Well, when Mr Morgan heard a noise or saw something suspicious, he'd come to the back door and shout at us.'

John Rhewys shook his head, laughing, 'Sometimes, he'd come after us. I'll never forget the times when we were running around that bank with Mr Morgan behind us. Well, we were quicker than him as you'd expect so he never caught us. He'd be going one way, and we'd be running the other. And sometimes he'd be around the back of the bank and we'd be by the kitchen door. It was open, of course, because Mr Morgan himself was out. Ivor used to nip in then, as long as the cook wasn't around. He had plenty of nerve.

'One time he got in when they were going into prayers. Nobody noticed him, so he hid. They had prayers every evening at Cae Gwyn, taken by Mr Morgan. Everyone had to go. Well, there was a beautiful roast duck just out of the oven sitting in the middle of the table.

'Ivor was hungry, of course. He hadn't had anything since breakfast. We'd come straight up from work, met at the top of the village and walked on up the hill as quick as we could.

'Well, he took a little piece of skin off the wing. It tasted so wonderful. Roast duck! He'd never had that before. He took a piece more, then the whole wing. Next thing he knew, most of it was gone.

'"No point in leaving just a little bit," he said to himself, so he finished it all, every scrap. When the cook came in and saw just the bones on the dish, she went to Mrs Morgan and told her the cats had had it.

'Ivor was always getting in. Another time he got in late at night when most of them had gone to bed. He'd just found the girl when he heard the cook, Mrs Little, in the passage. She had a fierce tongue when she found you. "Quick," says the girl,

"Hide in the larder. She won't be going in there again tonight."
So in goes Ivor – anything to please.

'Well! He'd never seen anything like it – so much food. They were having a big shoot at Cae Gwyn the next day. There were several big game pies with beautiful pastry flowers and things on top, a ham as large around as a butter churn, a whole side of beef, and jellies and custards and all sorts of sweet things. It was a feast!

'When Mrs Little saw the girl hanging around near the larder, she sent her off to bed and then locked the larder door. She was afraid of anything going astray. There was so much food all prepared in there. So she left Ivor locked in with the ham and all.

'He waited a bit, but the girl didn't come back and he couldn't get out. He had nothing to do – it was cold and there was the smell of all that food. Suddenly he started eating. He ate a whole game pie and started on the ham and the beef. When the girl tiptoed back down, she found him fast asleep. I don't know what he hadn't eaten.

'She didn't know whether to laugh or cry.

'He got into some peculiar spots.'

John Rhewys started to chuckle. Soon he was shaking with laughter.

'One evening, he was standing talking in the kitchen when he heard Mrs Morgan in the passage. Tap, tap, tap on those old stone floors. There wasn't time to get out, so he jumped down behind the clotheshorse that had sheets drying on it in front of the fire.

'She kept on talking, telling the girls this and that. She was talking about us too – telling them not to get caught by those bad fellows outside. Ivor enjoyed that, but then he thought she'd never go. If she'd have stayed a minute longer, he said, he'd have had to push the whole thing over. It was that hot.

'His face was as red as a hot coal when he got back outside. "Duw, John! I thought I was roasting in hell!" he said.'

Ivor married the girl the next spring, so he didn't have to go to Cae Gwyn any more.

A few months later, John Rhewys was returning from chapel in the evening. It was almost dark as he came up the hill by Cae Gwyn. Suddenly he heard a terrific noise in the lane. He couldn't make it out – it sounded like donkeys braying but, as he came over the brow, he saw it was Ivor with Mr Morgan and his daughter Lily.

Ivor had just told them about hiding behind the clotheshorse when Mrs Morgan came into the kitchen. They were laughing, all three as if their sides would burst.

We both laughed until the tears began to roll down John's wrinkled cheeks. From that time on we seemed to be fast friends. I went back several times to see him. Sometimes he went over his favourite stories, usually he told me new ones about humorous characters and incidents from his youth. But there always seemed to be something more that he wanted to tell me, something more serious, but which he still hesitated to say. Perhaps it was something more personal, more revealing, about his family or mine.

The last time I went up to Mynydd Bychan, I found John Rhewys Morris standing outside in the yard. It was a summer day, but the sky was covered in fine cloud so that a dazzling white light came down from every quarter of the sky.

I walked across to speak to him, but as I got closer I could tell that something was wrong. His face was still fine and distinguished, but I could see he had no idea who I was, and yet he hardly seemed confused as he gazed up at the round hilltops behind the barn. He merely seemed to be looking for something he had forgotten there.

4

With a Voice like God

THE LLOYDS OF Cildaugoed have the reputation of being the oldest family in the village. They had lived in Tremeirchion for so many centuries that no one knew when or how they arrived. Because of this, and a philosophical leaning in the family, they gained a spokesman-like authority in the village. When I moved into my cottage on the side of Sodom, this long line of meditative farmers was headed by one man, Dai Lloyd, who was well into his seventies. He was considered to be the best storyteller in the village, but no one encouraged me to call in.

Dai lived alone on a farm which went by the name of Cildaugoed, which translates as the retreat or nook between two woods. The farm is built defensively on top of a rock. The wall leading up to it contains massive stones, the size of megaliths, lying side by side. It is the site of an old kiln which may date back to the time of the Romans, who built a large fort somewhere near here in the first century AD.

The small rounded dome on which Cildaugoed proudly stands is the last rocky outcrop before the hills finally give way to the valley. From the road that runs just below the farm, only the pale grey barn is visible. Its walls of rough limestone boulders are windowless except for the narrow slits made for ventilation, and to provide a breeze to blow the chaff away from the grain when winnowing was still done by hand.

This long building housed everything from farm machinery to milking cows and their calves, and the hay, straw and grain harvested to feed them every winter. Around the outer wall of the barn great piles of manure had accumulated opposite to each door. No modern manure collection or dispersal had been implemented. The piles of cow droppings and straw slowly decayed and, as water seeped through the piles every winter, nutrients gradually leached out into the sloping pasture below.

Below Cildaugoed spread rich pastures and arable land, with fields of wheat, oats and barley, known here in combination as 'corn'. Green in spring and gold in September, each patchwork piece was marked off by an edging of trees containing oaks which had grown with straight, tall, wide trunks, unblemished by wind or competition. 'Marvellous oaks, but how could you get them out?' Dai grumbled.

Along the edge of a couple of fields, just below the farm, ran two tracks of massive limestone slabs. They were the remains of Roman roads which took the Romans up and down this valley and across to the now missing fort.

When I first called in on Dai Lloyd, one wet and windy early spring night, my car skidded and bumped up the steep yard. Unlike most other yards in this area, which were made up of cobblestone or cement, this one was formed by a sheer slab of rock that rose with alarming abruptness to several jagged rock flakes, before the yard finally levelled off towards the house. There were no lights showing anywhere, but as Mr Lloyd was an old man I thought it unlikely that he would have gone out on an unfriendly night such as this.

I entered the front porch and knocked on the heavy old door. Nothing happened. I tried again and then, as my eyes grew accustomed to the dark, I could see the porch was hung with cobwebs, and a fine dust lay evenly over the slate flagstones disturbed only by my own footsteps. No one had passed this way in weeks.

I walked quickly into the yard again, reassuring myself that this must be the front door for special occasions of which there hadn't been any recently, but I couldn't see another door. One side of the house abutted the hillside and was blocked off by a long open shed. The other was joined at right angles to the long windowless barn. To go around this barn meant walking right down the yard again and out into the field. I started through a doorway of the long barn. It was pitch-black. As I turned to leave, my face collided with a musty old sack.

Unnerved but not giving up, I walked all the way down the yard and climbed over the fence into the field. No sooner had my boot touched the ground than I sank up to my knees in old manure. It had lost its pungent smell from age, but not its fragile texture. I waded from one stack to the next in waves of frustration, anger and finally laughter.

At the end of the barn I finally saw a dim light. I had reached 'the back'. As soon as I knocked, I could hear a chair scrape back over the hard floor. The short, thickset man who opened the door showed neither pleasure nor surprise to see me and wandered immediately away to a single chair at a small high table in the corner. He seemed to be expecting me. Had he heard me at the front door?

I closed the back door and sat down more abruptly than I intended in one of the two remaining chairs which stood on either side of the room by a small fire. The seats of both were close to the floor, the legs having been cut down many times to even out a wobble or a broken leg. It gave Dai an instant advantage on his uneroded chair. In the grate a few coals glimmered, but gave little warmth.

This small back kitchen was apparently Mr Lloyd's living quarters. The spindly-legged table at which he sat was the cheapest of its type, made about ten years before. In one corner there was a sink of the same design that is often used in outside dairies. The only other piece of furniture was a small low chest covered by a red woollen blanket. The room was lit by one bare dim bulb hanging from the ceiling.

Without almost any prompting, Dai began to speak. To start with he talked about the First World War, but he kept returning to the present.

'They have no faith – that's the trouble now. All coming and going – to the town and back again – never staying in one place – the radio, the television.'

He shook his head and stared down at the tabletop which was covered in pale yellow Formica. Then he mentioned the name of Lester Jones. I had heard this name often. Everyone old enough to have known him, and even some who were not, would sigh and say, 'Ah! Lester Jones,' and shake their heads or add a few words of praise, but no one had been able to give me the least sense of this vicar.

'Lester Jones!' Dai Lloyd muttered. 'They buried him one cold day in that bad winter of thirty-three or thirty-four. Frost and deep snow everywhere.'

Dai's eyes opened, amazed. He was looking at the great snowdrifts.

'If it had been a better day, it would have been a great funeral, one of the greatest there'd ever been. Everyone would have come.'

His arms spread out to welcome a crowd, while a smile flickered over his face.

'They used the old hearse – rickety old thing – drawn by a horse – the one they kept fussing over in church meetings. They kept it in the coach house next to the old school, and that roof was falling in too. Should have taken better care of it. Then they kept arguing about who was going to repair it and how much it would cost. In the end, they got it done for eight shillings and sixpence. It was so old no one knew when it was made. The Salusburys gave it to the village, and they haven't

Tremeirchion church was built inside a roughly circular graveyard indicating that this was an ancient religious site. The unique name for this village may have originally described 'the cell of Marcianus,' a holy man of late antiquity.

been seen here since 1850. They burnt it after they buried Lester Jones. Just drove it down the hill to the old quarry and set light to it. It made a blaze, alright. Lester Jones was the last to be carried in it.

'You never knew him,' he said, looking at me with evident pity. 'Phuh!'

He was quiet for a moment, then he started in a low voice.

'He came to Tremeirchion during the Great War. I'd gone, but they wrote to me about him. I was in Egypt with all the flies. Never volunteered. Would you offer to go and leave your land to fight a war halfway around the world?'

His voice had grown loud and fierce, but he didn't stop.

'I wanted to stay here and look after the farm. They gave exemptions for farming, but they took them away after a while.

'We were four brothers – no girls in the family. They sent all of us, but Tom got a medical discharge. He'd never been well – he had no strength. I was the only one that went abroad that came back. We would have had a fine farm here, but after the war there was only Tom and me of the young uns.'

He stopped again, trying to remember what he'd wanted to say.

'But Lester Jones kept on going through it all. He helped people stay together. He kept the village together. You know what – they repaired the whole church during the war. It was in a terrible state. The roof was leaking and ivy growing everywhere, breaking up the mortar and water running down the walls inside. But when we came back it all looked spanking new. I always wondered who they'd found to do it.

'When the war was all over, the children heard about the armistice first because of the schoolmaster. He followed the news. Well, they made a band – used whatever they could find, bottles and cans and rulers, and one or two who had a mouth organ. They went playing right through the village down to Plas Newydd to tell Lester Jones the war was over.

'I remember when I saw him first in the village. He looked remarkable straight away. Tall and quite thin. He was talking to some people outside the Salusbury Arms. He was leaning over, but I saw the gleam – there was so much light in his eyes, and determination too.

'Then came all the sickness. Flu they said it was. Another death every day. There wasn't a family in Tremeirchion that didn't lose one or two.'

Dai raised his hand high as if about to strike someone, then let it sweep the air. 'Death – it came right through the village. But he kept on visiting people. I don't think he was afraid of death.'

Mr Lloyd looked at me with something close to a smile.

'All the maiden ladies were after him. He had invitations to tea all the time. He was a fine-looking man. Some of them never gave up hope, but he wasn't interested in all that. For him it was the church and the singing. When he came here he started the Tremeirchion Male Voice Choir with twenty voices.

You know how they sing even now. Well, in those days, if you went past the old school on Wednesday night, you'd think the windows would fall out. But it was beautiful! The boys from Elwyd Uchaf were good tenors. You can get basses any day, but Robert Owen from Tan-y-Bryn, he was a great bass.

'In next to no time, they were winning prizes around here and even a long way off. It was competitive then too. There was a farmer in the next village who'd go around with a wagon collecting all the best voices he could get for his choir – and they didn't all come from his village. But it was Lester Jones who got the Chairs.'

In Wales, Chairs made of seasoned oak are awarded as prizes to symbolize the customary enthronement of the finest poet and singer in a competition, and, in ancient times, their elevation into the Celtic priesthood, the Druids.

'He took them to all the competitions they could reach. They won more Chairs than anyone then. Lester Jones inspired them. But there was one memorable time when he'd taken them across the moors to sing. He landed them there safe.

'They were going to sing one of the Advent hymns. Well, just before they went onto the platform to sing, he said to them, "Take a big breath before that last line because you are going to raise your voices right up to heaven."

'When the time came, they took a huge breath, all together.'

Dai smacked his hands together.

'Crack!

'The stage went down and they tumbled through, piano and all – just as they were singing, "Cwyd ni tua'th orsedd fry [Raise us to thy glorious throne]."'

Dai chuckled, 'The boards couldn't hold them.' But then his face suddenly turned bitter.

'He tried with everyone, the children and the old people – but there was too much drinking then. The Salusbury Arms was open all day long. People going on a spree all the time. I remember Royal Roakes Day. Came once a year in the summer. They held it in the field opposite the Salusbury Arms. They had a brass band with I don't know how many trumpets – came specially from the coast. Games and cakes and things. A man from Brynmawr brought a Knock Down Sally. He had to ask me not to play any more because I'd won so much. But there were others going on a spree. To and fro across the road all day long.

'By the end of the day they didn't know where they were. There was too much drinking then. You can't drink and work. A lot of farmers gone to the bad. Fallen in with the wrong companion. Then what happens to the farm? It happened all over Tremeirchion. They didn't even go to church. They had no faith and they lost what they might have had. They should have stayed to hear Lester Jones.

'I'll never forget him in church on Sundays – especially when he was up in the pulpit. There was something in his voice, you couldn't help listening.'

Dai shook his head, annoyed that he couldn't find the words he needed until he finally stopped with a stony, quiet face and said, 'He had a voice like God.'

An important piece of the past in this village fell into place for me. Impossible, but I knew what he meant. Back at my cottage I wondered if Dai was the descendant of the poets and minstrels of medieval Wales, or even one of the ancient Druids who had a stronghold in North Wales. Or that he had just taken up this mantle.

'They transferred him in twenty-eight and then again later, down to the coast. Evan Davies, who came here later, was a curate with him at the end.

'It was the middle of the bad winter of thirty-three and terribly cold. Lester Jones didn't arrive for the early service. Mr Davies waited and waited till he couldn't hold it up any longer. Then he took the service, reading through it as fast as he could. There were only a few, but he didn't stay to shake hands after.

He was hurrying over to the vicarage. It wasn't even close by, but several streets away.

'When he got there he found Lester Jones sitting in a chair downstairs with his great coat on. Nobody knows how long he'd been like that.

'"I don't feel well," he said. "It is cold."

'"You should be in bed, Mr Jones," the curate said, just from looking at him.

'"Well," he said after a minute or two, "You'll have to help me."

'It wasn't easy. He was a big man and poor Mr Davies was quite small. But they got there somehow and the curate gave him some brandy. They were neither of them drinking men, but no one objected then. He died the following day.'

Dai paused. It seemed he had been drawn into a story he wished he could forget.

'They brought him back to Tremeirchion because they said that's where he'd been the longest. He had no family to speak of. But he belonged here. They buried him by the path going into the church.'

He said it with fierceness rising in his voice. Dai returned to the silence from which he had been aroused an hour or so before. Lester Jones retained the enigma that he had had, it seemed, as much in death as in life – but at last I felt I understood why this country community hung so tenaciously to his memory.

I rose to leave, but Dai stopped me. 'No,' he said with the first smile I had seen playing just at the corners of his mouth, 'I think you should go out by the front.'

With which he became very gracious and escorted me through into a narrow hallway. In the dim light I could see the gleam reflected off some well-polished, old oak furniture. Dai tugged at the stiff old door until it grudgingly opened wide.

5

Catching
hold of the axle

'BUT CATCHING HOLD of the axle – that was the best thing. We'd
wait for the carriage coming down the hill past the school. It
had to slow up then because of the drop, and we'd stop there
quietly until they'd gone by and then run like wild things after
it. It was a game to see who could hold on the longest.'

Miss Parry's eyes shone, catching the glow of her small fire
in the dark front parlour. She had always been spoken of as a
pillar of respectability, someone you could count on, but this
sparkle made me see there had been a time when she had run
like a wild thing. Now she stayed home warming herself and
cooking on one of the last small open cooking grates that was
still in use in this corner of Wales. Just like the one that now
stood cold and dusty in Penuchaf.

'Didn't you get dirty?'

'Of course, we got dirt plastered right up us into our eyes
and hair and everywhere and then there was always trouble.'

The hitherto gentle old lady beamed triumphantly. The dirt
and the danger were all part of their reckless act of defiance.

At that corner every coachman had his hands full. The
road coming down from the hilltops levelled off going past the

church, but just as it passed the school it dropped over the last and worst precipice – a drop that was barely negotiable with a horse and carriage, and was challenging on foot or even with a car today. It was here that the children exploited the coachman's distraction and chased wildly after the carriage, endangering themselves, the coachman and his horses.

But what else did these children have to do in a small Welsh village at the beginning of this century? The school in Tremeirchion was an ancient one – it had been started by a bequest of twelve pounds left by a lady of the parish to educate twelve indigent children, thus starting the first village school in the whole of North Wales. Even in 1700 that sum didn't quite fit the bill. The first school was built using the ancient churchyard wall for one side of the long low building. This school didn't last long; it went up in smoke, but a new one was quickly put up on the same site. It was this school that I remembered as a child, with its tiny mullioned windows peeping out from under a steeply pitched slate roof. The soft limestone mortar had washed away, leaving great age-darkened crevices in the walls. Such a building was not to the tastes of Victorian times and so, in the 1860s, the villagers were invited to subscribe to the building of a new school.

The new school, which stands just below the old churchyard, consisted of just one room, no longer than the old one but more than twice as high, made of precise machine-cut blocks and ornamented with cast-iron fretwork along the top of the roof ridge to exaggerate its height even more. The old school blends in with the ancient wall of the churchyard that dates back before the Norman Conquest, but the walls of the new school made of precise machine-cut blocks could have been built anywhere in England, or Scotland. It flaunted the new technology of the Industrial Revolution and the wealth that could afford to build so high and yet still have a few pounds over from the twelve hundred they had raised.

Things Welsh had reached a new low in the opinion of

One of the carriages that Sarah Parry risked life and limb to catch hold of – my great-grandfather's victoria arriving at Nantlys around 1900.

the British government. Welsh education had just been investigated and roundly condemned. A large portion of blame had fallen on the ancient Welsh language and the stubborn survival of the independent Welsh culture which was alien and incomprehensible to men in London.

Some schools were very badly managed, and the school in Tremeirchion in the 1860s was certainly no example of academic excellence. The school was run by a William Ellis, who was judged by the commissioner who visited the school to be ill-qualified for the post which he had already held for thirty-five years.

Mr Ellis must have spread his few talents too thin; not only did he play the organ in church, he was also the parish clerk and unique in these parts for being the only schoolmaster who

51

also ran the village pub. It's surprising he had time to do any teaching at all.

The only record, apart from Mr Ellis's own hastily scrawled logbook, is the report of the commissioner who visited the school when only forty of the ninety-six pupils on the books were present. That wasn't, in fact, a poor figure for attendance in Tremeirchion, even forty years later. Few children attended school full time.

The commissioner, John James, reported that the pupils who were there that day were 'extremely respectful' in their behaviour. From that point things declined. He found that not one 'could think in English, but about twenty knew a little common talk'. Twenty-four could repeat parts of the catechism, but only ten 'could read with ease', only seven could answer anything about geography, only three 'were beginning to learn the History of England', only two knew anything of mathematics and, of the twenty-four who could quote parts of the catechism, only two were judged to be well informed on the scriptures and only one solitary pupil could, in the opinion of this commissioner, write well.

Of the buildings he was complimentary, but reported that there was no sanitation and the furniture was in bad repair. His comment, at the neighbouring school of Bodfari, revealed one of the problems of Welsh schools: 'The master is a Scotchman. He was trained at Battersea. He questioned the children very sensibly and corrected every mistake which they committed in reading. He does not understand Welsh, and the children do not understand him.'

In fact, most of the learning of the forty scholars was probably owing to the Sunday school, which must have been taught by someone else because, of the one hundred and fifty on the books, one hundred and forty-six were there when the inspector came. No wonder Mr Ellis's pupils did well on their catechism.

Following the publication of the Royal Commission report,

an act was passed in Westminster that decreed that Welsh could not even be spoken in any school. In many schools after this, any child caught speaking Welsh was made to hold, or worse wear, the dreaded Welsh Not, a piece of misshapen wood. The child who was unlucky enough to be wearing it still at the end of the day was given extra punishment.

There is no mention of the Welsh Not being used in Tremeirchion, but English was enforced here too. The standard of education did not improve. The report for 1860 was a little more favourable, but things quickly deteriorated again until, in a rare move in March 1891, the incumbent was sent packing. He was replaced by Harry England. His name would have been enough to alarm the poor Welsh speakers in Tremeirchion. Mr England wrote in the school logbook, 'Took charge March 2nd, 1891. Master's desk and cupboard in utter confusion. Registers and weekly summary not touched. Daily attendance register simply is an apology for one.'

The next week he noted that the first week began well enough and that the attendance was 'the best all year'. Mr England took his job seriously. He had no sympathy for the muddle he found in Tremeirchion. He was determined to retrain all of the young minds he had been put in charge of, but he discovered that the children of Tremeirchion were a moving target. The attendance at Tremeirchion became a major preoccupation for Mr England, so much so that for the rest of his time in the village he went to considerable lengths to find out just why so many of his pupils weren't in school, and, as he did this, he left behind a picture of a child's life before the First World War in this area.

On his pupils' side, curiosity to see the new teacher quickly subsided, and alarm at his new regime took over. Mr England was a square, heavy man with a carefully trimmed handlebar moustache and small, sharp eyes that could stop any pupil dead in his or her tracks. Attendance was down the following week, and down again the next week until, by the end of the first month, Mr England was forced to note that attendance had been the worst all year. Even the pupils who had been faithful to the old schoolmaster had started to stay away.

The following month the scholars were examined by the Diocesan Visitor who stated politely, 'Grammar viva voce good. In other respects the schoolwork was deplorably bad and the poor little infants knew next to nothing.'

For all his stern discipline, Mr England seemed to be losing the battle against literacy, at least in the English language. It is possible that teachers in Tremeirchion had defied the government instructions and continued to teach in Welsh, in which case Mr England must have put the children into shock.

Then the weekly notes in the school logbook began to change.

'One scholar died of influenza, others look very delicate.'

By 1895, Mr England was observing the health of his pupils with the same care he put into his attendance notes. In October he noted, 'The attendance has slightly fallen; sickness has something to do with it, but several of the scholars are irregular in attending,' and again, ten days later, 'Many scholars are absent this week through illness – bad colds, in consequence the average has gone down, and is rather low. Satisfactory progress is being made with the standard of work among those present.'

But it wasn't just bad colds. In November he wrote, 'The attendance has fallen very low. This is undoubtedly owing to the prevalence of Whooping cough. Those children present are continually coughing and at present the outlook is serious.'

A few days later the so-called managers closed the school. It remained closed for five weeks and reopened on 20 December, but the health of the thirty-nine pupils who came to school that day caused the school to be reclosed for another three weeks. On 18 January, after two months, the school was reopened when Mr England noted, 'The closets were emptied, cleaned and sweetened and the schoolroom scrubbed and washed.'

Mr England and his wife had begun to involve themselves with the health of their pupils. Some pupils walked two miles across the hillside to school, and if it rained or snowed they had no rubber boots. Trevor Jones, who had walked all the way from Sodom, remembered, 'Just little leather shoes that didn't do much of anything for you. But it was nice when you got to school. Mrs England'd dry you out. She'd take you in the house and put you in front of the fire, with nothing but a shawl over you. You didn't have to go into lessons till your clothes were dry, just sit there by the fire, drinking hot soup!'

Another time this same group of children were chased by the pigs from a smallholding they had to pass through. The strange old lady who lived there let her animals roam freely and scavenge what they would. This time the pigs tried to see what they could get from the children. In their fright, the children dropped their satchels of food.

'The pigs ate our lunch – paper and all, but it was alright because if you hadn't any lunch Mrs England'd feed you.'

Judging from the logbook, ill health, even death, haunted the pupils of this school throughout the winter months, but if Mr England counted on better attendance as the weather grew warmer in spring, he hadn't caught up with the reality of a farming community. In 1895, no sooner had outbreaks of measles and scarlet fever died down, than Mr England felt obliged to report, '24 April. The average this week is lower than that of last week... this is partly owing to potato planting.'

And again two weeks later, 'Although the number on the books has risen to sixty-five, the average has fallen to forty-six which is very bad. Potato planting not quite finished and turnip and swede sowing [in progress].'

In June he observed that, 'The bigger boys [are] going to

pick fruit in the [Seminary] College gardens,' and in July, 'Average much lower – most probably in consequence of the hay harvest.'

And the following week, 'Hay harvest still in full swing.'

During the corn (or oats and barley) harvest, which was the most labour intensive event in the farm year, it was considered inappropriate to ask children to attend school at all, and the school was duly closed for four weeks, starting on the date the corn or wheat first ripened in the parish. Even in the winter months, there was still some money to be made from casual labour.

'October 1894. The bigger boys have been enticed from school by the Head Keeper of Bryn Bella, who employs them watching pheasants.'

When I read this record I didn't see the irony of it. I was as innocent as Mr England.

And then, throughout the year, there was Denbigh market.

'The attendance this week has been very good and would have been better still but for the bad effect Denbigh market day always has upon the attendance.'

One conscientious scholar, Richard Hugh of Penuchaf, used to combine helping on the farm with attending school. At regular intervals throughout the year, he used to bring several lambs down the hill to the village pub, which stands close by the school, on his way to school. Richard Hugh seems to have loved school. He earned a prize for perfect attendance year after year.

But, during some bitter weather at the end of one November, Mr England noted, 'This week's average best of current year. It is a most extraordinary fact that the best attendance occurs in the hardest weather.'

The farming year was over and the school boasted a good stove. The weather outside was wretched for the handful of children who wandered the hillsides when they should have been in school.

Given all of the frustrations that ooze out of the pages of the school logbook, it is all the more remarkable that the hitherto scathing inspector from the diocese would remark in Harry England's third year at Tremeirchion, 'This little school is exceedingly well taught, and has passed a very good examination.'

The results in drawing were better still. Four years after Mr England took over the school, he wrote in the logbook: 'Feb 14th. The Drawing report was received on Tuesday morning, mark = excellent. This is the fourth time for the school to receive the excellent award for drawing.'

Drawing was good, and music and art were even better.

'Singing has been successfully introduced, and the diagrams prepared by the master to illustrate the Drawing Lessons testify to the presence of unusual ingenuity and intelligence in the teaching of art.'

Mr England seems to have been a musician and artist at heart. He wasn't so imaginative in other areas. The government inspector commented that reading would improve with better books. School reading books in Great Britain were stunningly boring right into the 1950s. How breathlessly dull they must have been to get a bad mention in 1898!

A frustrated artist deep down, Harry England was remembered vividly by Trevor Jones, Bluebell, who told me,

'He was very keen on music. He was a good composer, and no copyist either, taking a bit from here and a bit from there like some people. They were all his own. I'll never forget the singing. After break in the afternoon, there'd be no more schoolwork, only singing. He had us singing Welsh airs so that we got right inside of them. I only knew him later on. He'd been at the school for a long time and got gentler, so they say, from how he started.'

This diminutive, but kindly, builder would never say a word against anyone.

'I was a bit of a joker so they said.

'Mrs England would say, "Trevor doesn't have to say a thing, his eyes do the talking."

'Now, if you were clever you could get Mr England off the subject. And once his foot was up on the desk, we could sit back. You could put your books away because he'd be telling stories for the rest of the lesson. He used to tell stories about his youth in South Wales. He told one about how his grandfather was "pressed" for Waterloo. He was just coming home down the road when the militia came by. His family didn't see or hear from him again until it was all over.

'He used to tell jokes too. He had one about how the first steam engines in South Wales had funnels made of bricks that they could dismantle to go through the tunnels.

'I think it was the war that softened him, seeing his boys out there doing the fighting. Right through the war, he'd read the papers to us every day and his talk was always on the war. I think we knew more than the people who were running it. We must have known where every dugout was.'

When the news of another local casualty reached the village, Mr England, always the careful record keeper, went back to the old school register and wrote into the book, next to where that pupil had last attended school, the date he had been killed and the battle where he had fallen.

As the law demanded, inside the four walls of the school Harry England spoke English and nothing else. However, as soon as the children spilled out into the playground, they instantly reverted to their mother tongue. Harry England followed them and, outside the walls of the school, he gave them pointers on how to improve their spoken Welsh.

6

Tom and Jo 'y go"

RISING ABOVE TREMEIRCHION to the north stands the loaf-shaped summit of Moel Maen Efa. For thousands of years this dominating heather-clad hill boasted a great megalith, 'a stone standing on its head'. It was erected by people of the late Stone Age. There are still plenty of megaliths in Wales, but what was unusual about 'Eve's Stone' was that it carried a biblical name. Beliefs around the stone must have survived into the Christian era, and someone thought it prudent to put the big stone onto the map of the new religion. Accordingly, Maen Efa was christened with the name of the woman who first led man astray.

Maen Efa has gone, destroyed no doubt in the nineteenth century when these stones were mistrusted in the false belief that they had been erected by Druids. On the lower slopes, surrounded by thick woods, the Jesuits maintained one of their few houses in Wales. Since 1662 this zealous Catholic order owned a small farm with a meadow known privately as The Priest's Field. This piece of land apparently supported a priest, who kept up appearances as a small farmer while feelings against the Roman Catholics ran high.

In the nineteenth century the huge seminary of St Beuno's was built on the land and became famous as the training ground of Gerard Manley Hopkins, who wrote one of my favourite poems, 'Pied Beauty', while there.

Glory be to God for dappled things –
  For skies of couple-colour as a brinded cow;
    For rose-moles all in stipple upon trout that swim;
Fresh-firecoal chestnut-falls; finches' wings;
  Landscape plotted and pieced – fold, fallow, and plough;
    And all trades, their gear and tackle and trim.

All things counter, original, spare, strange;
  Whatever is fickle, freckled (who knows how?)
    With swift, slow; sweet, sour; adazzle, dim;
He fathers-forth whose beauty is past change:
          Praise him.

Hopkins' 'firecoals' makes me think he warmed his winter hands by the glowing forge of the smithy on the road below St Beuno's.

The seminary required all their employees to be or become Catholics. One of these was Joseph Hughes, a young blacksmith from a Non-conformist family. Sarah, his wife, was nominally Catholic too, but she rarely attended mass in the seminary chapel. Their children however became Catholics and, in the early years of the seminary, the whole family became the butt of anti-Catholic sentiment, including one incident when stones were hurled at the smithy.

Soon after he arrived at the seminary, Joseph Hughes was given permission to build a house for himself alongside the road which leads north out of Tremeirchion. During the day, while Joseph was at work, Sarah walked to the quarry where the stones for St Beuno's had been blasted out of the hill. On each trip she collected any rejected blocks and loose stones that she could find, and then carried them a full mile back to the smithy in her coarse apron. When the pile outside the smithy was large enough, Joseph set to work. Late into every evening after he finished his smithy work, he slowly built

The stable and forge where Tom and Jo worked at Henafon.

Henafon, a four- or five-roomed, two-storey house, entirely from the stones Sarah had carried. After such a life, Joseph fell ill and died while his sons were still young men.

The seminary was unwilling to hand over the running of the smithy to Joseph Hughes' sons. Ivor, the eldest, was twenty-eight, but he had already gone to work at the seminary farm where he would become the shepherd caring for the sheep on Moel Maen Efa. Tom, the next son, was twenty-four, and Jo, the youngest, was only nineteen. These two, Tom and Jo, were skilled at smithy work long before their father died. They had grown up helping him. When his health made it impossible for him to work, they worked the smithy by themselves. They were skilled enough to take over, but Jo, like his mother, did not attend mass at the seminary chapel, and Tom had acquired a reputation for practical jokes.

'One day, when the doctor had come to see his father, Tom came in and saw the doctor's cape and hat hanging by the door. In a flash, Tom threw the cloak around his own shoulders and

61

pulled the hat down as low as he could over his face. It was a magnificent long wool cloak and Tom went down the path all bent over and muffled up. Then he climbed into the doctor's carriage and muttered 'Hafod-y-Coed', still keeping his head all bent over like this.

'Well, the carriage went off with Tom in the back enjoying the ride. Then, just as they pulled up at the front door of Hafod-y-Coed, Tom put his head out of the window and said all cheerful-like, "Well now, I think we'd better be going back for the doctor, don't you think?" The poor coachman could hardly believe it – that he'd had the great fat blacksmith from Henafon in the back for the past half-hour instead of the doctor.'

Like Lester Jones, Tom and Jo Hughes were known and remembered throughout the village, but most people, on hearing their names, would only shake their heads at the same time as grinning broadly. The only person who described them in detail was John Rhewys Morris of Mynydd Bychan. He knew the family well because he worked at the seminary farm along with the eldest of the three brothers, Ivor, who was the courting companion of his youth.

The only other person who told me much about Tom and Jo was Mrs Jones, John's daughter, who still lived at Henafon, the house her grandparents built. As soon as I explained to her that I was collecting the old stories of Tremeirchion, she became excited.

'There's so much to be told,' she blurted out, her eyes shining with emotion. But, in spite of her enthusiasm, Mrs Jones did not tell me much about her uncles. Like everyone else in Tremeirchion she preferred to tell the story of another family. Of Tom and Jo's jokes, she only said that Tom 'was always telling yarns to the boys'.

John Rhewys was one of these boys, but he claimed he could tell the difference between Tom's stories, the ones that were true and the ones that weren't, but only because of Jo.

Whenever John Rhewys arrived at the smithy, Tom would have a new tale to tell. One time when he came down to the smithy, Tom asked, 'Well! Well! What do you think happened to me this morning, John?'

'I don't know Tom, do I?'

'Well, I was busy in here shoeing, when up comes a horse and trap – and who do you think was in it? Lester Jones and three parsons, all dressed from head to toe in their long black robes. Lester Jones steps towards the smithy with the others all following behind, and then says to them all, "This is the smith I've been telling you about!"'

Tom had beamed from ear to ear when he repeated what the clergyman had said.

'"There must be something to me now, mustn't there, with four parsons all coming to see me in one day?" Tom had demanded.

'I couldn't do much but agree,' John chuckled.

But the seminary wasn't impressed, and turned over the running of the smithy to Edward Jones, who sent out important-looking bills on good paper under the heading:

To Edward Jones, Coachbuilder and Wheelwright
All kinds of repairs neatly and promptly executed.

but the bills were receipted,

Paid Thomas Hughes
With thanks

Tom and Jo were a powerful combination. Ivor had left the smithy to them, and Edward Jones soon followed his example. The seminary had little choice by then but to accept the partnership of Tom and Jo. From then on the bills went out under the simpler, often handwritten, heading:

T. & J. Hughes Blacksmiths

That is, if they had a heading at all. Tom often used just a piece of lined paper, torn off a pad.

Bills were sent out only in the official language of the time – English, but to all the locals they were 'Tom a Jo y go', using the Welsh.

'They made a great team,' John Rhewys said one day.

'They were laughing and joking all the time they were working. Tom was always in a good mood. He'd be telling a story and then he'd say, "Isn't that so, Jo?"

'Jo wouldn't say anything. He never could tell a lie, not even for Tom, but then he'd never say that Tom was lying, either. Whenever Tom was telling a story, you had to watch Jo and that wasn't so easy because he'd be bent over with the horse and there'd be all the smoke about. But sometimes, if you were lucky, you'd catch Jo with a queer look, his lips all buttoned up. It was no smile, but you could tell he was trying to hide one. Then you knew Tom was pulling your leg. You could never tell from looking at Tom. His face'd be as straight as a poker. And still you could never be really sure, but some people couldn't tell at all.

'One day, Aneirin Jones came to the smithy with the groceries. Now Aneirin was very serious – all business. He owned a big shop in St Asaph, but he delivered the groceries around Tremeirchion himself. He knew everybody, but you could never get a smile out of Aneirin. And yet Tom was always watching people going by, assessing characters. That's what made his jokes so funny.

'Well! This time, when he saw Aneirin coming up the path, Tom stepped back out of the smithy. His face was all pulled down as if he'd had a bad shock.

"'Ah! A big job in Sychdyn!"

"'Oh! What happened, Tom?"

"'Richard Lloyd! He sat down just this morning to eat his breakfast and, would you believe it, it was all over by eight! Such a nice man. I can't believe it!"

'Aneirin dropped his groceries and rushed back to his trap. He was off in a flurry. Mr Lloyd had been one of his best customers.

'He'd been to several houses and passed on the bad news, but he wasn't watching the road too closely. Suddenly, he came around the corner, and his pony nearly ran into Richard Lloyd bringing the horses back from ploughing. Aneirin's eyes nearly popped out. He was too flabbergasted to even say good day.'

Death was a frequent theme for Tom. One time he hinted to a carpenter that an old woman with a particular reputation for shrewishness had finally died. The carpenter set off immediately to measure up for the coffin. As soon as the door opened, he began to explain his mission until he realized that the old woman was on her feet in front of him.

The one subject Tom kept well clear of was sex and the dealings between men and women. He never married or showed any interest in doing so. Remaining single was not unusual in Tremeirchion, where siblings often stayed together as none of them could afford to leave or share out the family home. Tom and Jo, with their smithy business, could have afforded to marry, but two wives would have made it hard for them to stay on together in Henafon.

'They say Jo had a woman friend one time, but nothing came of it, of course,' John Rhewys said with a meaningful smile.

From a photo of Tom and Jo outside the smithy when they were already middle aged, it is clear that neither of them were good-looking men and never had been. They were both huge – they weighed between eighteen and twenty-one stone in the opinion of their neighbours, or three hundred pounds, more or less, depending on who you were talking to.

Farmers prided themselves on being able to estimate 'live weight', but Tom and Jo's size seems to have confused their well-practised eyes. They were both over six feet tall and Tom's face particularly matched the massiveness of his body; his cheeks were large, square and flaccid, but he could turn his drooping oversized face to any expression, particularly astonishment and innocence. With his larger-than-life expressions, he kept his audience on tenterhooks. His ability to keep a straight face was legendary.

Mrs Jones said that Tom was a diabetic, though he never received any proper treatment.

'He wouldn't go near a doctor if he could help it. One year, he sat in a chair for two days with a broken hip before he'd go to the hospital. And his toe – he had a problem with his left foot. He never let a doctor look at it.'

In spite of Tom's handicaps, Tom and Jo were master craftsmen.

'They were the best smiths for miles around and they were fast too. They worked together on each horse. Tom would be heating the shoe in the forge and hammering it out on the anvil, while Jo would be clipping and filing the hoof. They were the fastest smiths I ever heard of. They could shoe a horse in twelve minutes. Most smiths take four times as long.

'And they were strong as well. People would travel for miles to bring them a horse that was too wild for anyone else to shoe. They had some fierce ones too! Tom would just mutter, "And now, we'll settle you!" Then he'd lift up one foot and Jo would take another and not let go. Well! The horse couldn't go far – it had only got two legs left. They weren't hard either. I never saw them twist a horse's lip.

'Tom was that strong that he could lift up a donkey and carry it in his arms. One time, a man drove over in his trap, but the pony was so scared and jumpy it wouldn't leave the road to come up to the smithy. The owner was cursing and pulling and pushing, but Tom didn't want to wait around, so he went down and lifted the pony up and carried it back to the smithy. That man never came back – he didn't like to think his pony was so small.

'They were popular, though. There was always a line of horses waiting outside and plenty of farmers sitting on their backsides in a cart having a laugh. It was a gathering place. People got together, swapped stories and jokes, but you didn't get much done on the farm that day.'

Tom used to travel with the stallion from Brynllithrig, Mr Platt's prize horse. When the stallion went around all the county shows, they took Tom along too. One time, when they were down in London, Tom entered a competition for farriers.

'He won first prize against the smiths from all over England – he was better than all the rest,' John Rhewys beamed, as if Tom's accomplishment had lifted up everyone in the village.

'He wrote out his bills beautifully too! He took trouble with them – they were a work of art. I had a friend here once who asked if he could take one back to show a man in Birmingham. And Tom had no more schooling than the rest of us – and that wasn't much!'

His niece remembered,

'After Tom died, we found all his books. A whole roomful. He had a record of every job he'd ever done – and so many accounts unpaid. Tom never would ask twice for payment and he never refused to do something for anyone on account of their not having paid. You'd never have looked at a farmer's son then. They were so poor and so 'digalon' [disheartened] – afraid of their own shadows. That's changed at least.'

Dai Lloyd of Cildaugoed remembered Tom and Jo most for the commotion that broke out at the smithy in the summer of 1914.

'When the war came, they gave Tom an exemption for the smithy, but they said Jo had to go. As soon as he heard, Tom went into a fit of activity. He went to see people and wrote letters, but they said Jo had to go like everybody else. And so, off he went, but Tom wouldn't rest, he kept writing letters.

'Right through the autumn there were more and more horses outside the smithy. You had to see it to believe it. If you went past Henafon there'd be a line of horses down the path into the road, around the corner, and all the way up the hill to the road to the seminary. That's quarter of a mile of horses, if not more! I can't imagine where they all came from!

'And Tom kept writing letters saying he couldn't manage – he couldn't do the smithy by himself. Then, before Jo's lot went overseas, they let him out. He was the only man I ever heard of that they let out again before he'd heard a gun go off. Suddenly it was all like before, and Tom and Jo were just the same.'

Soon after the war ended, Tom and Jo bought a farm on the mountain, Pant Glas, an old house with two stone barns and a few fields amounting to about fourteen acres. It was an isolated farm; the nearest neighbour was the Jones' of Penuchaf, who lived about a third of a mile away across the fields.

Tom and Jo's father, Joseph, was born and raised less than a mile from Pant Glas. Perhaps Tom and Jo thought they would go back to the mountain one day, or perhaps they just wanted to do a little farming. Possibly, too, they were hoping to escape the watchful eye of the seminary.

One of their neighbours on the mountain remembers seeing them driving up to Pant Glas.

'They looked such a sight – I'll never forget it! They were the first fellows in the village to buy a car. They had an old Morris Oxford with two seats – you could open the back and put two in. Well! You could hardly see the car, they were both so big! They were like two boulders balanced in a wheelbarrow. It's a wonder how the car got up the hill.'

But, most of the time, Tom and Jo were down in the smithy, with Tom up to his tricks as usual.

'Most of the beer that was drunk in Tremeirchion was brewed at Price's Breweries in St Asaph. Well, for many years, Price's sent out a lad with the deliveries. He was deaf and dumb, but he could whistle. You used to hear him coming down the hill by Henafon whistling all the way. That's how you knew he was coming – by his whistling.

'He used to come up to the smithy to bring the beer and collect the empties – those big old stone jars. Well, one time, when the boy was there, Tom lifted an empty gallon jar to his mouth and pretended to drink, then he made a terrible face like only he knew how. He dropped the jar and gripped his stomach as if he had a dreadful pain. The following week the boy brought him a new cask of beer for nothing.

'"And yet I never asked for it," Tom said. "I never told a lie." That was part of Tom's cleverness. He knew how to mislead you with the truth. He always knew what was going on,' John Rhewys said.

'One Christmas the bailiff at College Farm had a friend come to stay. This friend said to Mr Rees that, more than anything, he'd like to hear a party of Welsh carol singers because he'd heard so much about the Welsh melodies.'

Welsh religious tunes were usually composed of three, four or even five entirely different singing parts to make up a very complex harmony. It is said that in the past the Welsh had so few musical instruments that they developed their singing to have the richness and complexity of a choir with a full orchestra.

'Well, Mr Rees went to see Tom Edwards and asked them to sing. They were a noted family of singers and it was all arranged. They were to come down to sing at Sychdyn and Mr Rees' friend was to give them a gold sovereign. Only Tom found out about it and asked if he could go too, but Mr Edwards told him "No".

'Now, there's a door in the back at Sychdyn, and Tom was on the lookout at Henafon. When he saw them going down the lane to sing, he followed quietly across the fields. Then, as soon as he heard them start to sing at the front, he went and knocked at the back door. Someone handed out the sovereign and Tom went off.

'They kept on singing at the front. They sang and they sang, just waiting for the money. Eventually one of them went to the door. "Oh!" they said inside. "The money's been given half an hour since."'

Apparently, Tom kept the money, and no one grudged it.

Everyone liked Tom. Mrs Jones did not want to discuss Tom's jokes; she preferred to remember him as he was when all the farmers and horses had left at the end of the day.

'Tom never went anywhere much after he stopped travelling with the stallion. He was always at the smithy. After work, he'd wash up and put on a clean shirt and then he'd sit on the bench outside the smithy with Jo. People would stop and have a chat. Pass the evening talking.

'Jo would go to the pub for a pint sometimes. He used to play buttons – which hand held the button. If you got it right, the other fellow would buy your pint. Suddenly, one day, Jo fell ill. They took him to the hospital, but he was dead the next day. Tom never slept well again.'

John Rhewys, who remembers this time well, told me,

'There were no more tricks after that. Tom wouldn't even smile. He was a broken-hearted man. He had a motto he used to say, "Dim byd ond heddwch" – nothing more but peace.

'Jo died in January and, as soon as he was gone, Tom said he couldn't manage the smithy by himself. So David Jones, his brother-in-law, came in to help. They worked together for just over a year. It was August the year after Jo died when Tom didn't come down early like usual. David called up,

'"Are you alright, Tom?"

'"I'm fine," Tom shouted back.

'But when David went up, he found Tom dead, lying on the bed. Just like Tom – even in the end he couldn't say it straight.

7

Savage Williams

ONE OF THE entries in the burial register at Tremeirchion Church for 1916 starts normally enough: 'Thomas Williams – The Union Infirmary – March 27th – aged 67 years.' It is written in the vicar's best copperplate script, but Lester Jones couldn't leave it at that. No one would recognize the man he had just finished burying by his real name, and so he added lightly in pencil, 'Tom'. But that was really no better, and so the vicar put church decorum aside and added the name by which this man had been known as far back as anyone could remember – Savage.

Lester Jones didn't do so well by entering the Union Infirmary as Savage's 'abode'. The fact was that Savage had no home, and he would have hated it to be thought – quite incorrectly – that he had died at 'the Union'. But Lester Jones could scarcely write the truth.

'The St Asaph Union Workhouse' was the full and accurate title for 'The Union', but no one ever used it because the reality of the 'workhouse' was so hated and feared in Tremeirchion and every other village. In this area, the workhouse was most often referred to as 'Cartrefle' which means, literally, 'home place', which was the politest description anyone could find for this place of poverty and degradation.

Savage Williams wasn't his name by baptism. He was christened plain Thomas Williams, but Savage's father had himself been given this strange name when he was baptised, and, in Wales, a person used to be known not so much by their first and last name but by their first name and what was most particular about their lives, their farm or their trade. In this family what was most unforgettable was the name 'Savage', and so the boy was always known as Tom Savage, meaning 'the boy belonging to Savage'. But as he grew up, his reputation grew to match his strange name and his first name all but dropped out. He became known as Savage Williams himself, or just plain Savage, because, 'he was a violent man. He scared people. You had to be careful with Savage.' Dai Lloyd spoke with caution in his voice as if I still might meet him.

Savage had grown into a huge, lumbering man. Almost everything about him was clumsy – he even caught his breath in uneven short, sharp bursts. His moods were unpredictable. In his youth he had been violent. No one provoked him later on – even though he had harmed no one in years. He rarely got the opportunity because almost everyone let him come and go as he pleased – except at the workhouse where he was treated with the same cold disapproval as all the other inmates.

Savage was an 'itinerant' – as they were known by people who shrank from the reality of these people's lives. They were otherwise known, by people more familiar and less scandalized, simply as tramps. Some people called them vagrants, but Savage wasn't a vagrant. A vagrant was someone who belonged to no parish. Savage belonged to Tremeirchion, and no one denied that.

Savage Williams was born in Tremeirchion in a tiny hillside cottage known as Tŷ Gwyn, which means literally 'white house', which made Tremeirchion forever after responsible for him, according to the Poor Laws first passed in the time of Elizabeth I. Each parish was required to care for its own, and so Tremeirchion was responsible for Savage, even though he had had no regular bed in Tremeirchion or anywhere else since his childhood.

Since 1601 the law had identified two types of poor people: 'the impotent poor' or people with physical and mental handicaps which made it impossible for them to compete in a hard world, and 'the able-bodied paupers', all the rest who seemed just too wayward to accept the strictures of hard work for low pay. As far as the law was concerned, Savage was an able-bodied pauper and, as such, was given the minimum provision provided to any group.

'They were stricter then, too,' Trevor Bluebell assured me. It didn't take much to become unemployable at a time when jobs were precious and employees 'dutiful'. If anyone didn't conform there was no safety net, except the workhouse – and that wasn't a soft landing. It was intended to be uncomfortable and unattractive, the worst of all possible options – and it succeeded.

The elegant front of the St Asaph Union Infirmary contained the rooms used by visitors, the master of the workhouse, and the board of guardians, which was made up of local landowners and dignitaries. Behind these half-dozen plastered, decorated and furnished rooms lay the workhouse itself. The main service

The front rooms of the St Asaph Union Infirmary were faced with Anglesey marble in a style that could have graced the front of a grand house.

rooms, for eating and sleeping, were arranged in the arms of a large cruciform, well concealed behind the pretty building in front.

In these rooms there was no lighting or heating – just a few fireplaces that were rarely, if ever, lit. Inmates rose and went to sleep by daylight.

Between each arm of the cruciform was a closed courtyard – one for men, one for women and babies still being breastfed, one for boys and one for girls. On reaching the workhouse every family was separated. Only babies being breastfed were allowed to stay with their mothers. And mothers and children were one of the most common groups to arrive at Cartrefle: mothers with one or two children, possibly pregnant again, 'deserted by husband', and the others, even more numerous, the single women pregnant or with a baby who no one would shelter now.

Children made up twenty-five per cent and often more of the inmates of the St Asaph Union Infirmary. Women and old people, another fifty per cent. And then there were people like Savage, known as the 'outdoor poor' – people who were capable of work but, for one reason or another, didn't manage to support themselves. These outdoor poor were not expected to stay at the workhouse, just to rest for a few days before going back into the outside world again, or at worst being referred to the next workhouse twenty miles away. There was an idea that, if they were kept moving, they might stop somewhere and get a job. These outdoor poor mainly lived by their wits in which society, wrongly, assumed they were lacking. Many were just oddballs – a mystery to almost everyone.

There is a story of one local tramp who arrived at the building site of a large new house a few miles from Tremeirchion. While he wandered from room to room looking at the work, no one paid much attention. He spent a long time looking at the men working on a 'complicated ceiling'. Nothing was going right.

Some of the elaborate casts being applied to the ceiling had fallen and broken, the others just didn't look right.

The tramp approached the foreman with what seemed an almost business-like air. He offered to do all the plasterwork. He'd done it before – not recently, but long ago. He'd do the ceiling, all of it, on one condition, that no one came near him while he worked.

The man who had shambled in had an air of authority now, a gleam of determination in his eyes. The foreman decided he hadn't much to lose. As agreed, the tramp locked himself into the room and came and went secretively for several days. When he emerged at last, everyone crowded into the room. They were shocked, it was so beautiful. The man took his money and wandered off, a tramp again.

The trouble was it was always hard to tell the difference between a tramp, who had dropped out of village life for his own reasons, and someone who walked the countryside looking for things to steal. (Sometimes they were the same people, often they were not.) Savage looked big and wild enough to commit murder over a few shillings or a matter of honour.

Many tramps came and went through Tremeirchion, some stopping off for a few hours and some staying on, lingering in the neighbourhood for several days or weeks. Others, a select few, belonged in Tremeirchion and that's where they stayed most of the year – living in the parish, never at their own family's farm but usually in a haystack nearby. At the turn of the twentieth century there were three well-known tramps like this in Tremeirchion. Each resided in a particular haystack, along with, whenever he could get it, his favourite form of alcohol.

There was Will 'Fres who slept in the loft at Henblas, and Bob Parry who stayed in the barn in Cildaugoed, and Savage who spent most of his nights in the haystack at Summerhill, the first farm at the bottom of the hill in Tremeirchion. Some people were frightened of these strange untidy men who would appear suddenly out of the darkness of farm buildings. But each farmer apparently decided they did no harm and would be an extra pair of hands in an emergency. So the tramps would work occasionally and be given food in return. They were like strange night watchmen – they would be the first to notice a fire in the stacks, and thieves and troublemakers were more likely to avoid the farms where these men slept, particularly Savage's domain of Summerhill.

The fear of strange or unknown tramps was one thing, but even in his own village Savage was given a wide berth. In his youth people had tried to bring Savage to heel by making him work and provide for himself, or at the very least meekly accept the meagre subsistence provided by the workhouses for the unemployable, but those would-be reformers had come off badly in the confrontation. By the late 1800s no one messed with Savage. If he chose to hang around at harvest time, he would be given a little bread with the other workers. If he did some work for a few hours he might even be given a few pennies, but no one told him he wasn't welcome and few people told him what to do. He had achieved a position of independence that few tramps ever reached. He was really master of his own life and destiny. In other villages, Savage might have been fetched off to the lunatic asylum, but Tremeirchion was used to strange characters and looked after its own.

Eventually, having walked the tightrope between what he could get away with and what would bring the authorities after him with dexterity, Savage overstepped himself. He intervened in the world of Anglo-Welsh landowners – and, even worse, when several of them had gathered together for a day's sport. Savage couldn't have found a better way to make so many powerful enemies in one day.

One of the favourite pastimes of the men from the large houses was going shooting. From the beginning of October to the end of January, when pheasants, the main gamebird of Britain, started to nest again, owners of neighbouring and even far distant estates used to (and for the most part still do) meet for shoots or shooting parties. These gatherings ranged from just a couple of men and two guns, to a large party of men from all the adjoining estates, and up to a dozen guns.

Whatever the number of guns, there were usually three or four times that number of beaters employed to beat the fences and trees to stir up game, stops or flankers (old men posted to stop the birds running out down the hedgerows), and pickers-up to collect the game. This large crew would be made up of estate employees, casual labourers and anyone else the keepers could rope in to make up the numbers.

These shooting days provided one, if not the only occasion when the richest people in the countryside would spend an entire day with the poorest men and boys in the neighbourhood. Both sides eyed the other with quiet suspicion. Rarely would a gentleman do more than nod his head towards a beater he knew personally. A beater had no right to open any conversation with any of the gentlemen.

On the day of a shoot, the beaters would be carefully positioned at the far end of each covert where game was thought to be sheltering. The guns would be positioned at the opposite end, about fifteen yards back from the covert, waiting for the birds to fly out.

Then, at a signal from the head keeper, each beater had to move forward. Each man had been given a line to follow, no matter what the terrain or undergrowth. On the way he was to hit every piece of wood – gate, fence, tree or branch – in the line of the path he had been assigned to stir up the game, and drive it towards the guns as well as alarm the birds enough to make them take to the air. All things being equal, pheasants are large and heavy birds and they prefer to walk, but it is considered unforgivable to shoot a bird which is still on the ground.

After a few minutes, or as much as an hour, depending on the size of the covert that was being beaten, the first pheasants would take to the air and fly out of the covert in front of the guns and the shooting would begin. As the first shots rang out, other game driven into an increasingly smaller range would fly, too, towards the guns. At that point there might be dozens of pheasant in the air, at the same time as hares and rabbits also breaking cover towards the guns on the ground. By these methods, on one well-keepered estate in Tremeirchion, there was a total bag of two hundred and seventy-eight pheasants shot on one day in 1887 among the twelve guns who attended.

After two or three hours of beating and shooting, there used to be, and still continues to be, a huge picnic lunch brought out for the guns. Large packs of beef, pheasant, ham and other sandwiches, meat pies, fruit, cheese and even desserts were transported in hampers and eaten in style on open hillsides on fine days. On cold winter days the guns would return to the main house for a hot lunch.

On one chilly day in the late 1800s, a particularly large party had gathered on a nearby lord's estate to shoot over Cwm mountain – an area of several hundred acres. It was going to be a full day's shooting and so lunch was served in a small keeper's hut out on the mountain. These huts were used by the keepers when they were out at night watching for poachers.

By the end of the morning there was a huge bag of pheasants – 'hundreds of them all lying on the ground' by the hut – a display of how successful the morning had been. Dai Lloyd grimaced.

The guns had all gone into the hut for lunch. Outside there was the usual motley collection of two dozen or more beaters, farmhands and schoolboys, with Savage among them. No one thought much of it. He came and went as he pleased. He blended in with the crowd there and he might even have been taken on as a beater for the day if the keeper had been hard up for spare hands.

But Savage was in one of his moods – he wasn't ready to stamp around the hillside beating a nine-inch stick on trees, fences and gateposts for the customary one or two pennies.

It was, in fact, considered an honour to participate in the excitement of this ancient sport. No matter how many birds were shot, beaters weren't given game in these parts.

The keepers were busy talking to the gentlemen, discussing the day's sport and, in passing, enjoying some of the grand lunch that had been provided. Most of the beaters were hanging around outside waiting for the gentlemen's lunch to end. The men who lived close by would have gone home for lunch, the others had to bring their own – bread and lard for the poorer ones, and bread with strong-smelling home-made cheese for the luckiest. It was soon eaten. Savage looked at the pheasants and must have thought it a shame that so much good food should be shared by so few. He started to wander to and fro, waiting for his opportunity.

When no one was looking, he snatched up a huge bundle of pheasants and hurried off through the scrub. But not content with that lot, he went back for more at least once, if not twice.

Somehow or other, Savage spirited every single pheasant away from the back of the hut. How he got two or three hundred pounds of dead birds down off the hillside is a puzzle. Either it was all planned in advance, with a donkey waiting close by, or he must have hidden them on the mountain and returned that night to collect his haul.

With the lengthy shooting lunch, the endless packages of food, pies, sandwiches and glasses of warming cherry brandy and the leisurely break afterwards, Savage's escapade wasn't noticed for nearly half an hour. The first people to notice were the keepers. Could the entire morning's bag be missing?

At first there was confusion. Had it been collected for transport back to the big house? Then the keepers noticed that Savage, who had been there at lunchtime, was also missing. If Savage had made off with a dozen pheasants or so, Savage being who he was, the keepers would probably have taken private action against him, and a deputation would have been sent to the haystack at Summerhill. But he had taken every single bird belonging to his lordship – and what was worse, the bag of all his gentleman guests.

Game had long been a sensitive possession, particularly in Wales and Scotland where few of the natives of the land were allowed to enjoy the wildlife from it. The large landowners who rented out their land, without exception, reserved the gaming rights for themselves and their guests. A farmer could have the land and labour on it to make it yield what it would but, every winter, if it held any wildlife worth mentioning, he could expect to see Englishmen in their country clothes striding across from one covert or copse to the next, followed by the usual motley collection of beaters and flankers and pickers-up.

It was, and continues to be on many estates, the last hangover from feudal times. All of Britain still legally belongs to the Crown. Early on, it was vested in the lords of the manor, but the Crown wanted to hold on to the right to pursue game. Owing labour and produce to the lord of the manor had been abolished long before, but landowners never relinquished the game rights to their land because, though it used to be hard to farm two thousand or more acres, it is no trouble to shoot over the best coverts of a huge estate each winter. This holding back of the game rights had long been one of the main grievances of rural radical agitation.

It meant that a tenant farmer could grow corn, turnips and hay, but he couldn't shoot any of the abundant wild animals and birds which sheltered in the woods and at least, in part, fed off his crops summer and winter. Only crows and blackbirds were classified clearly as vermin, since no landowner wanted to eat them.

Taking game was discouraged and punished by every means by most landlords. But Savage had not only taken game – he had taken the game that had already been 'bagged'. It was more than theft – it was an insult and a challenge to the powers of the neighbourhood.

Few local murders were investigated by the police more energetically and rigorously than this theft by Savage. It seemed that the entire local police force was mobilized to bring him in.

But Savage was canny and bold and his theft had, if anything, made him new friends in the countryside. In fact, he had become something of a local hero overnight, daring to stand up to the landlords and taking what many people said should not belong to them anyway. But even with that amount of support, the energy with which the police set out to find Savage made it clear that he couldn't stay in the neighbourhood. The police were asking questions at every farm and cottage that might shelter him.

He dispersed his large haul with remarkable ease and left the neighbourhood, travelling south through the hill country. Keeping to the wild hillsides and crossing valleys only under cover of darkness, he was able to travel almost the entire length of Wales, just as rebels against England had done long ago. Within a few weeks he arrived in a large mining town in South Wales. To keep out of the hands of the authorities, he abandoned his old ways and took a job in the coal mines – probably the first normal employment in his life.

It might have seemed that he was safe and that the trouble he had got into had pushed him into becoming a regular citizen after all, but the insulted gentry did not give up so easily. The police throughout Wales had been put on the alert for this pheasant thief and hunted him down to the mine where he was working.

Two policemen arrived at the pithead and demanded that Savage be brought up for arrest. Word was sent down to the coalface that the police wanted to see Savage at the top. Like a rabbit in a burrow, with all exits but one blocked, and that last one netted, it seemed that Savage was caught. But when he heard, Savage thought rapidly. He found the fastest and nimblest of his workmates and persuaded him to come up to the pithead with him. When the cage reached the top of the shaft, Savage saw just two policemen. As planned, his friend leaped out of the cage and raced down the hill, pursued by two surprised policemen. Savage left the cage and walked the other way, back into the hills and wasn't heard of again for years. Perhaps he decided that his fame had betrayed him. And yet, true to the traditions of his kind, he couldn't stay away for good.

Several years later, Savage slipped back into Tremeirchion and returned to his old haystack. Curiously, the police had no interest in the case any more. Perhaps the owner of Cwm mountain had died, and so Savage wandered the village just as he had in the past, but with even more swagger and authority than before.

Old Savage Williams had a unique standing now in the village – almost a Robin Hood reputation – but it didn't quite obscure the old Savage that everyone remembered. When a violent fight broke out between the farmer and his wife at Summerhill, the farmer's wife uttered a few parting shots and fled to the nearest person she knew of – Savage in the haystack. Suddenly, Savage was thrust into the middle of a domestic furore with tempers running full storm on both sides.

How would Savage cope? The farmer realized what an opponent he might have taken on. Savage climbed down from the stack and said gruffly to the now apprehensive couple at the bottom, 'It's not my business.' The couple, in their surprise at themselves and Savage's quiet self-possession, promptly stopped fighting.

Many of my earliest rides on the mountain led back home over a slippery bridge made out of a couple of planks that cross the little stream that tumbles down the slopes from Penuchaf farmyard. By the time it reaches this crossing, the stream has cut a thin gorge. The grassy slopes above drop all but perpendicularly down to the stream, which runs over the rocks and between the trees in the bottom of this cleft. A little further down are caves occupied thirty-five thousand years ago by some of the first members of *Homo sapiens* to reach Wales.

Hardly any sun reaches this bracken-filled valley, and there is a chill sombreness about the place. I don't know if that coolness is there anyway, or has been there for me ever since John Lidford told me that a tramp was found there one winter lying face down in the icy water of the stream. It was Savage. Had he fallen – his mind sodden with drink or obscured by illness? Or was he just leaning over to drink and slipped?

He had been admitted to the infirmary at the workhouse a short time before for reasons that are unrecorded, but he had left again as soon as he could.

Although he had the security of the infirmary, he was probably dying and knew it. He would no longer be able to wander as he wished, and so it seems he came back to this little valley which lay just below the house where he was born and, with his customary boldness, lay down in the icy stream. No one would want to take their last breath in Cartrefle.

8

Building the hall

THERE'S NO MISTAKING when you've reached the valley. Everything changes in the space of a few yards, the line of a major fault line. The steep slopes give way to an undulating plain, large fields filled with agricultural crops or lush green grass, each field marked off with thick hedges or copses and woods. In this fertile plain, wave after wave of people from England settled, including my own great-grandparents who built the large country house where I lived until I was eighteen.

In fact, my family is neither English nor Welsh, Irish or Scots, but a jumbled mixture of all of these. Both my mother and father were descended from some of the famous Welsh princes, but my mother never thought of that. She considered herself English from top to well-heeled toe. She missed the world of her English, and even colonial, childhood in what was then Persia. She reared us to think of ourselves as English, nothing else.

My father never made speeches about this to us, but he told us often of our different ancestors, including Llywelyn ap Iorwerth or Llywelyn the Great, though he always referred to him simply as Llywelyn, as if he was a familiar uncle. He puzzled all his life about where his *plas* or home close to our

Meyriel Edge

A statue of a boy holding a giant fish stood in the centre of a small lily pond where goldfish were quickly consumed by the local porridge-coloured newts.

house had really been. As soon as I was old enough, I decided I was Welsh, a stowaway in our grand English-style house.

As a child I revelled in the peacefulness of the spacious garden. My sister and I played on the wide gravel paths that wound around the house; we peered into the flower beds which held spikes of sapphire-blue Anchusa and golden daisies that towered over us. We climbed the tall conifer that bent over if you went too high, and explored the old greenhouses and outbuildings with scarcely disturbed remnants of Victorian England, old horse harnesses and bamboo chaise longues on wheels.

Inside the house we wandered through an Ali Baba cave – there was always something ancient to rediscover, chests of drawers full of darkened photographs, sealing wax to close a letter, Edwardian haberdashery, costume jewellery. There were old sewing boxes, tripods to hold candelabra, with gilding falling off the unctuous caryatids, pictures, letters and books – books by the thousand – hundreds and hundreds of obscure titles that would never be seen in a library again. I devoured many of these books, and spoilt my interview at one university by citing the obscure juvenilia of Lord Byron among my recent reading.

But the older I grew, the more I wondered at it all – this huge house and just four or five people sleeping there each night. Between meals you never saw another person. There were rooms that no one had visited for weeks – or months – where one could find complete peace. Then my sister and I heard about Penny Black stamps and decided to make our fortune from an old chest of deeds. We found dozens of Victorian stamps, but no Penny Blacks.

Instead, we came across delicate tracing paper, beautifully drawn and inked. We looked at the tiny writing. These were the plans for our home, with every detail drawn in and the purpose of each of the forty rooms clearly labelled. This was the house as it was intended to be.

The plan began to make sense. It was the blueprint for a self-contained community, with rooms specially designed for every activity. There was a high-ceilinged laundry building with enormous coppers for boiling the sheets, and a large room for drying and ironing. (These rooms had been converted into garden rooms, with fitted mirrors and cabinets to display the next generation's china.) There was a dairy for making butter, a small brewery for making beer, and a bakery with an old-fashioned bread oven that was large enough to hold three children.

There was even a set of rooms built just to separate the ash and cinders from the thirty-four coal fireplaces. In the wall of the first room the ashes were placed into the open end of a large sloping cylinder, which crossed through the second room and opened into a third. When rotated, the ash fell between the bars of the cylinder and collected in the second room while the 'clinkers', used on the muddy paths in winter, slipped down and dropped into the third room. This sequence of rooms was, by itself, as large as a small city flat. My aunt told me that when the house was built someone was employed just to make and keep all these fires burning.

I had always been a little ashamed of my home. Why was it so big? Most of my friends lived in normal-sized houses. I had lots of questions, but behind them all my sister and I loved this eccentric oversized house because it was so solid and peaceful when little else about our lives was. I became curious about my great-grandfather. His full-length portrait gazed kindly over us from one end of the dining room. Though more ancient ancestors were often talked of, Philip Pennant was rarely mentioned in our family, except to strangers who enquired about the building of the house, and then we would hear again the curious chance of his great inheritance.

Philip Pennant was not born wealthy. His father was an English clergyman, respected and respectable but lacking any fortune to share amongst his nine children. Philip wasn't even the eldest. He was the fourth son, but, at the age of nineteen, he became the heir of a great house and estate belonging to a Welsh family that had been famous in North Wales since the Middle Ages.

This ancient family was known for having produced a father and son who became the abbots of Basingwerk. Thomas Pennant had found celibacy not to his taste and so left the abbey to marry the lady he loved. His son, Nicholas, who succeeded him as abbot, was less particular; he remained abbot while fathering many children by different women. He is said to have entertained so many friends at the abbey that they had to have three sittings for each meal. His extravagant life was brought to an abrupt close by the dissolution of the abbey by Henry VIII in 1536.

Far from giving up with the dismantling of the abbey, the former abbot instead pursued his own interest more aggressively. He seized what he could of the abbey lands and decided to capture what was now the leading ecclesiastical appointment in the area – as vicar of Holywell – despite the fact that there already was a new vicar. He pursued the new incumbent with a posse of henchmen equipped with bills, bows and staves until the poor man fled for his life and the former abbot seized possession of the vicarage. Some of the ancient lands that Abbot Nicholas grabbed were ultimately inherited by my great-grandfather in 1853.

But there was a catch. This branch of the once over-powerful family had shrunk to just one girl, called Louisa. By the will of her grandfather, if she died childless, all the family property was to go to his godson, my great-grandfather. In 1854 Louisa died in Rome of 'Roman fever'. She had no children.

Her husband, a viscount, was, however, far from willing to relinquish his wife's wealth to this young outsider, and so a legal battle raged for six years until a settlement was finally reached. My great-grandfather agreed to give up his claim to all the ancient family property, including the great house of Downing with its valuable furniture and books and the old abbey lands, in return for inheriting everything that his Pennant godfather had acquired in his own lifetime, which included farms and houses scattered across North-East Wales and one notorious pub.

When my great-grandfather finally came into a good part of his inheritance, the powerful families of North Wales rushed to console and befriend the new heir. In spite of his recent losses he still seemed to have almost everything a man could wish for. That same year he married the daughter of a local family who was descended from some of the ancient royal lines of Wales. All that Philip Pennant lacked was a prestigious house to go with his new position in life – the young couple had nowhere to call their own. They took out a long lease on an exquisite Italianate house in Tremeirchion, and slowly began to make plans to build their own house in a similar position looking west over the valley half a mile away.

In the autumn of 1869 Philip met the architect Thomas Wyatt at his London office, and Mr Wyatt travelled to Wales to inspect the proposed site of the new house. My great-grandfather didn't need to go into much detail of what he had in mind – he trusted Wyatt, who came from a family who had designed many of the landmarks of Victorian London, including the extravagant St Pancras Railway Station.

My great-grandfather mentioned a figure, around £7,000, as the amount he wanted to spend on his new house. A few weeks later a preliminary sketch arrived at his Bryn Bella home, with front and back elevations and a ground plan for a modest country house embellished with Renaissance-style ornamentation. My great-grandfather was content. He was interested in things that were functional and this seemed a practical plan, but his young wife was not so easily pleased.

And what made it even more difficult was that she couldn't say exactly why. Thomas Wyatt moved the three main rooms, the large classically proportioned drawing room, dining room and library around within the structure that he thought could be built for Mr Pennant's price. But, when the third detailed plan fared no better than the previous two, Wyatt abandoned all his previous restraint and allowed the house to balloon out around a three-storey 'open glazed court' in the middle of the house to provide light for all the enlarged rooms and additional passages. Wyatt saw that his clients wanted something huge, so now he was beginning to think big.

On the outside, the ornamentation – which had been quite noticeable on the first plan – hadn't increased, while the surface areas of the brick facades had grown by more than half, with the result that Nantlys has less variation of texture and decoration than many factories built at the same time.

Wyatt added an enormous mullioned window looking out on to the court. With its central stained-glass panel displaying the family crest, this window extended upwards for two storeys, casting a bright red, white and green light into the interior of the house. The 'glazed court' became one of the most attractive, if impractical, features of the house. By the time I came along,

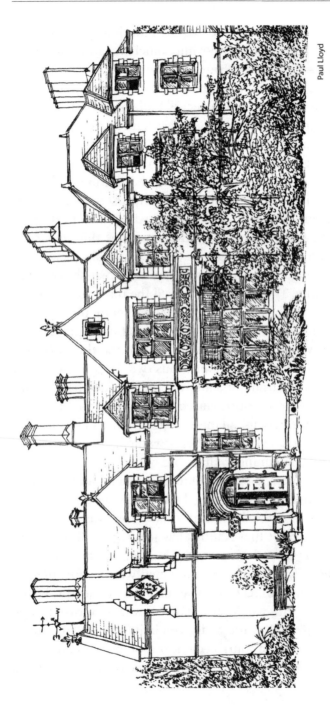

Paul Lloyd

The main façade of Nantlys looked out across a long park leading up to what we knew as 'the mountain'.

it had been allowed to fall into disrepair and siphoned heat out of the centre of the house in summer and winter alike. But, for all that, it cast a bright airiness right into the middle of this ponderous house.

It was one thing to plan a house on this scale but yet another to work out how to build it, and to bring in the necessary materials from the new station in Bodfari. Everything for the house had to be transported by horse and cart. Wyatt probably made only one more visit to the work site. The onus of deciding exactly how to get the plan built fell on his assistant, a Mr Allen, who travelled to and fro from London, keeping Wyatt informed on progress to the house. Allen was assisted by the on-site supervisor, Mr Jones, who was employed to make sure that there were no disastrous misunderstandings between the Welsh-speaking workforce and carters and the London architect.

The basic materials for the bricks were literally dug out of the ground within a few hundred feet of the kilns nearby. The clay was simply spaded up from the field itself (a large shallow pit still remains), while the sand for the bricks was quarried from a seam of flame-coloured sand only a hundred feet further down the valley.

Even the limestone for the thousands of feet of mortaring was produced in Tremeirchion. Great blocks of stone were blasted away from the side of the hill half a mile from the brick kilns. In order to render this limestone into lime to make mortar, Philip Pennant financed the construction of a large limekiln at the rock face.

In December 1871, the meticulous accounts show that Edwin Williams, a carpenter, was hired to make the 'moulds, tables, wheelbarrows, etc.' and two large kilns to fire the bricks were constructed. The heat from these kilns was so great that it baked the surrounding soil. On winter days, looking out from my bedroom, I could still see the two large dark circles when the field was ploughed. The finished bricks were trundled up the last couple of hundred yards to the site of the house in the wheelbarrows made by Mr Williams. Joseph Jones, who continued working for the family until the 1920s, remembered working 'as a boy bringing the bricks up in a wheelbarrow'.

By midsummer 1872, there were four separate teams at work on 'the new mansion house', the brick-makers, the men working at the quarry and the kiln, a local Welsh contractor, John Hughes of Holywell, employed to build 'the carcase' of the house, and another contractor from Chester to do all the fine details in the important rooms.

In 1874, irate letters began to reach my great-grandfather, along with bills from contractors and suppliers not involved with the house. It emerged that John Hughes had fallen into debt and was rebuffing his creditors by telling them that he was owed vast sums by the English gentleman for whom he was building a great mansion in Tremeirchion. This kept his creditors at bay for a time, but as 'the English gentleman' never seemed ready to settle his arrears, one after another of the creditors lost their patience and started writing directly to my great-grandfather.

By the time he heard about it, tempers were already running high, and his surprise and claim to be fully paid up was disbelieved. No sooner had one batch of creditors been finally convinced that they had been taken in, than a fresh batch arrived. There was a simple way out of the jungle of accusations – to fire John Hughes – and many men would have taken that route, even sued him for defamation of character, but that wasn't my great-grandfather's way. John Hughes apologised and stayed on. He was even given an additional contract and he served my family well. Nantlys stood virtually as it was built for one hundred and twenty-five years.

The house and surrounding buildings took exactly 890,000 bricks to build, almost all of which were made on site. The total cost of construction was just over £13,000.

Thomas Wyatt handed over to Mr Allen, and Mr Allen to Mr

Paul Lloyd

The complex maze of roofs above the kitchen didn't provide easy access to the gutters, which soon filled with leaves, while thousands of bees moved in.

Hughes before construction was complete. Unfortunately, his exacting supervision was needed a stretch longer, as one of the final walls did not have a foundation.

By the time I was a child, huge colonies of bees had established themselves in the roof space above the kitchen. In the summer, when the sun came out, the garden was thick with the humming of hundreds of thousands of bees, who loved the rambler roses and clumps of lavender lining the paths.

Finally, in the summer of 1875, the front rooms of the new house were painted in 'crimson lake', a deep, dusky red rose that was fashionable at the time. With hanging oil lamps and oriental carpets, it made the household interiors look more like the halls of ancient temples. The entire service area of the house was painted a practical spartan grey. The dichotomy between the main rooms for entertaining and the 'back' of the house could not have been clearer.

Outside, the gentle slope of the land was interrupted to

Paul Lloyd

When I was a child, the house looked out over a grass tennis court-cum-croquet lawn and, in June, a bank of dog daisies tall enough to hide tortoises and terriers alike.

make a large terraced lawn, which wrapped around two sides of the house and terminated in a wide moat-like ditch or 'ha-ha', so that the view from the house would drop from the smaller upper lawn to the broader longer lawn below and then continue uninterrupted down the long sloping field below and out across the valley.

Large quantities of evergreens and beds of brightly coloured annuals and perennials were planted all around the house to compliment the bright red brick facade in the style of the day but, in spite of all this, the house looked like an enormous beached whale in the peaceful surroundings of the fields until the trees, including one copper beech and a giant sequoia, grew in this sheltered spot to huge specimens.

Beyond the long wood that bordered the house on the north, a kitchen garden exactly one acre in size was laid out, with alleyways lined with dozens of espaliered Cox's Orange Pippin apples and delectable pears. On the north side a long high wall was built to support and ripen fan peaches and nectarines.

One thousand pounds was spent on landscaping, stable buildings and the walls that surrounded almost the entire one-acre garden around the house. At that time a four-room house in Tremeirchion could be built for just twenty pounds.

The London architect was long gone by the time the garden was constructed. There are no plans or correspondence, but Mr Hughes from Holywell did not betray my great-grandfather. He kept the brick kilns fired up to provide thousands more bricks for high walls and low walls all around the garden. Where walls were not wanted or needed, he made thick gates and a deep west-facing moat or ha-ha. Every inch of the perimeter of the garden was built securely to exclude a gardener's greatest challenge in North Wales – rabbits.

These outer walls, stout pine shutters, bars and locks speak eloquently of an age of fear and insecurity, and the gulf between my family and our neighbours. According to the accounts, the final cost for building this remote, strong house was £13,044.19s.6d. – nearly twice the original budget.

When the newly-married couple had first settled at Bryn Bella, advertisements were placed for servants, ranging from a coachman and footman to a lady's maid. Dozens of neatly written letters arrived from all over the country, but very few were from experienced, well-trained staff, who usually stayed where they had first been employed. And so Mary Pennant found herself interviewing a collection of willing, but inexperienced young people. Philip selected a butler called Robert Williams from Flintshire, and Henry Rees, a relation or friend of his, who was only seventeen, as footman, and a coachman named George Bevan from Shropshire.

For a cook my great-grandmother took on a stout and firm Scottish woman from Surrey, Anna M'Crae, and firmest of all, one Elizabeth Hook, a nurse from Gloucester. Miss Hook was already aged forty and experienced in dealing with children. She was the oldest and most experienced member of the nine-strong live-in staff. Of the rest, four of them were under twenty, and not one of the nine were married. By the time the new house was complete, designed to accommodate the family and guests so spaciously, and fourteen to sixteen live-in servants, there was not enough money to employ such a large staff – and, even worse, my great-grandmother had proved unequal to the task of managing a household. My great-grandmother was a hard taskmaster. She wanted total obedience, even subservience.

By the time the Pennants moved to Nantlys in 1876, only two of their original servants came with them – the unflinching Miss Hook, who no one dared to challenge, and young Sarah Ellis, a Welsh girl taken on as nursemaid but now grown with her charges to the position of 'schoolroom maid'. George Bevan, the coachman, Robert Williams, the butler, and Henry Rees, the youthful footman, had all gone.

My great-grandmother was a combination of opposites. She had wanted this great big house, but now didn't know how to manage it. She wanted to be so much in control that she inspired a secret rebellion among her large staff of live-in servants, and they became untrustworthy for being so distrusted. She then ended up ineptly trying to train the next round of novices, but when she was not struggling to be mistress of her small kingdom, she painted delicate and subtle watercolours.

The best hint of what had gone amiss in Bryn Bella was the elaborate provisions around the sleeping quarters for the staff on the third floor. The men were separated by a door equipped with a stout lock from the sleeping quarters of the women. Not only that, but there was also a three-storey stone staircase, known as the fire escape, built so that the men servants never had an excuse to pass the women's bedrooms.

In fact, there was only one man left to make use of the new spiral staircase. David Parry, known as a 'general', became the only live-in manservant, apart from a new youthful footman, known ominously enough as George Breeze, who slept on the ground floor next to the silver.

Many of the people who now came to work in this oversized house were not live-in staff from faraway, or even from the village of Tremeirchion, but women like Miriam Crewe who came to work in the laundry. Miriam just walked down the steep slope from the neighbouring hillside community of Sodom. She was known locally not for any skills with the bleach or an iron, but as a powerful soothsayer.

9

The people of Sodom

RISING UP OUT of the valley on the steep slopes near my old home, there used to be a community that was bizarre by everyone's standards – English and Welsh, valley dweller and villager alike. At the edge of this steep limestone escarpment the landscape changed within a few feet, from the sheltered luxuriance of the valley to the large empty spaces of the hillsides. A meagre close-cropped turf clung stubbornly to huge open pastures, which swept down the slopes marked off by untidy fences. Wire, new and old, stretched between odd hawthorn bushes and trees, all that remained of an old hedge.

Only in sheltered corners could trees grow to full maturity. The rest were short, stunted and misshapen from the prevailing winds and the slope they stood on. The woods were not woods at all, but sprawling thickets of impenetrable bracken and brambles in which only wild animals – foxes and rabbits, weasels and stoats and gamebirds – thrived. Even sheep got lost and stranded, and horses and cows broke their legs in the concealed rabbit holes.

The few roads that climbed into this wilderness either angled up the slope following the route of some ancient animal track – a challenge to anything on wheels – or climbed straight up each fierce gradient. These steep old lanes were made by people who didn't even have the use of a horse, because horses were a danger to themselves and their riders on such climbs. The roads were so old that they had worn down deep into the hillsides, turning into shady gullies with banks so high on either side that people and cars travelling along them disappeared below the level of the surrounding slope.

Every few hundred yards along the sides of these roads was a small stone- or turf-built cottage. Some have been renovated, modernized and re-inhabited, but many were abandoned, their walls of small stones and pebbles steadily falling back into the hillside from which they were gleaned long before.

Some of these houses and cottages have disappeared altogether, their stones taken to mend a nearby wall or make foundations for a road. All that remains are a few boulders lying under thick stands of bracken; the vanished houses are only remembered still because the people who lived there haven't been forgotten.

Just above the barn where my great-grandfather set up his estate carpentry shop, one particular hillside helter-skelter starts up the slopes. To test any but the boldest driver, it forks right in the middle of the steepest gradient. The right-hand branch angles across the hillside from there to a crossroads near the crest of the ridge. From this point you can see the old iron-age hill fort on Moel-y-Gaer, but no house is visible. This is the centre of Sodom.

The name of this community, which seems to have no inhabitants, still has a powerful effect on anyone who lives nearby. Some people laugh at the mention of the name; others are disturbed. Sodom drew me like a magnet when I was a child. I loved the feeling of timelessness on this wild hilltop and the puzzle of how Sodom had earned its strange name. I wanted to know about the people who had lived here, but there was almost no one to ask because, when I was growing up, cottage after cottage stood empty, abandoned.

The area had acquired the name of one of the God-forsaken

Michael Newbold

A view across the lower slope of Sodom towards the house occupied by Miriam Crewe, and the chapel in which Betsy Lewis attempted to bring some order.

cities of the Old Testament 'because of the quarrelsome nature of the people of the district', one local historian working in the 1920s was told.

Trevor Jones, Bluebell, said there was more to it than just a group of cantankerous hill dwellers.

'People ran and hid here. They were harder to find. This part was known for its rum characters.' He shook his head half disapprovingly, but had another thought. 'Of course, you didn't have to do very much to have the law after you in those days.'

On the shoulder of this steep ridge, Sodom seems to lie in a no man's land. It is, in fact, on the edge of the ancient legal jurisdictions of three parishes. Until around 1800, most of these summits were wild unenclosed common land. Then, as happened in many parts of Wales, the population rapidly increased and food supplies dwindled. Many families emigrated to the 'New World'; others moved back onto these hillsides where ancient man in Wales had always lived. They built turf houses and established permanent squatting rights. The big landowners followed soon after, claiming the large parcels in between. Too late, however, to prevent a large community of freeholders living in tiny cottages, often with no land, but owning their own front door.

Property ownership is still confused up here. There used to be large chunks of land that no one knew who owned. Sodom still remains something of a no man's land.

As a child I wanted to know about Sodom. I asked plenty of questions about who had lived up there and why, particularly to John Lidford, the teenager who lived on the fringe of this community and who was employed to ride with us over the hilltops. But although he would talk hilariously for hours about everything else, he wouldn't say a word about the hill people, except for the tale of one old man who had stubbornly refused to leave his tiny primitive hillside house. 'When he died they didn't find him for days,' he told us as we pored over the pages of old books still left in his little one-room house.

The only thing I learned about this area as a child wasn't actually true. I later learned 'old Gerald' had been towed down the mountain one snowy winter on an upturned bedstead pulled behind a horse. (The ambulance couldn't get up the hill.) After a stay in hospital he had become a beach chair attendant at a local seaside resort. He never went back to Sodom.

The wall of silence around Sodom was complete as far as I was concerned, but that didn't dull my curiosity. Then, in the early 1970s, the abandoned houses of the hillsides began to change. They were being demolished, and large new houses were being put up on their sites. In areas such as this, according to the Town and Country Planning Act passed in 1946, no new houses could be built – only existing houses refurbished. The law was passed partly to preserve areas of great natural beauty or useful farmland. The result was that, by the 1970s, the old tumbledown houses of Sodom became valuable house sites in spite of the wild precarious lanes that connected them to the valley floor.

Wanting to save at least one of these old hillside houses, I persuaded my father to give me one of the few that had ever belonged to our family – a house that had been abandoned like most of the others around 1954. It had stood empty for sixteen years – but was virtually unchanged, apart from many broken window panes and two big holes in the roof. One had been there so long that a hole had rotted clean through the floor of the bedroom beneath, and luxuriant grass was growing in the sodden timbers around the hole. But both holes were easily repaired and the house stood almost exactly as it was built just under two hundred years earlier. The roof was covered with thousands of tiny slates that, for the most part, had stayed there untouched and undamaged since the house was built. Thin oak pegs pushed through a hole in the top of each slate were hooked over the rafters and secured by strong lime plaster held together with horsehair.

As some of my city friends and I started work on this cottage fixing the windows and slates on the roof, people from the neighbourhood came up to see what we were doing. They were puzzled and amused that I, 'the daughter of the big house', was scrabbling around the roof of this derelict cottage. Strange and crazy as they decided I was to turn my back on the apparent luxury of Nantlys, their attitude to me changed. As a prospective inhabitant of Sodom, I was no longer simply one of the people from the big houses who were supposed to know nothing about how the rest of the village lived. Locals began to talk to me more. They'd stop for a chat, and chats in this rural area could last for hours.

In my preoccupation about how to anchor a ladder onto the steep roof, my anxiety about heights and my search for slates small enough to replace the missing ones, I hardly noticed that I had crossed over from being one of the English up here to being just one more in the long line of eccentrics who lived in Sodom. In the bare half-mile from Nantlys to Nantgwilym Uchaf, I had travelled a long way.

But it wasn't until I had unravelled the contents of Penuchaf and learned the stories of Tremeirchion that people began 'to chat' about Sodom. Even then, Sodom was a secret most people continued to pretend didn't really exist at all.

The people who would talk about Sodom were just four old men who had lived there most of their lives. There was Lewis Jones, a wild-looking, gruff man who was famous for retelling the old stories that he had heard as a child, stories about fairies and ghosts; and Dan Owen, who was completely blind and unable to study my face. He was never sure how much he could say, whether I was friend or foe. Old Mr Dyke was happy to talk but, as he had only moved to Sodom in the 1920s, he was just a newcomer. Finally, there was Trevor Jones, Bryn Ffynnon, who more than anyone on the mountain wanted to tell the whole story, wanted the story of Sodom to be written down and remembered, but even he kept worrying about who I was, where I had been born.

Only one of the old inhabitants of Sodom lived there still, but even in the 1970s, Tom Jones would hardly say a word about the place where he had spent his life.

How had anyone ever managed to survive on these bleak hilltops? Most of these tiny cottages had no land attached to them, only the luckiest had a few fields. When I started talking about the economics of Sodom, ignorantly I was close on the heels of what no one wanted to tell me. So each man worked a little harder to make sure I didn't find out what I seemed to be so eager to know. One after the other, they would cough, perhaps scratch their head, fix the fire and then start to talk about potatoes and turnips.

The Covells of Pant Glas, I was told, had had one small field where they grew turnips and swedes. Hugh Jones, Pen-y-Mynydd, used his only field for growing carrots. That made everyone laugh – I didn't know why but, though carrots grew well here, they were a particularly unsuitable crop for Sodom. The tiny farm where Lewis Jones' family lived 'had a little bit of everything, a couple of cows, some potatoes and turnips'. Many families couldn't even afford a cow, but nearly everyone had pigs. Pigs could exist on all sorts of scraps, and when there were no scraps you turned them loose to forage for themselves. Then, when you needed the pigs, you went looking for them.

Each autumn lots of pigs turned up in the long park that leads down to Nantlys. The driveway was lined with huge old oak trees – much older than the house but presumably marking the line of a hedge that was there before the house was built. Every autumn, when the acorns fell, a lot of stray pigs would suddenly appear in the park where they would stay until the last acorn had gone.

Mary Anne, Pwll y Carw, lived all her life on rabbits, according to Trevor Jones, Bryn Ffynnon. He always laughed hard when he thought about those rabbits and, as he laughed, he watched me. I didn't know it for a long time, but the word 'rabbits' was a doorway to the other world of Sodom – the reason why Sodom was so different. But, until I learned to laugh – not just a polite chuckle – at the first mention of that word, no one would tell me anything more. It was, in fact, a password and, until I knew it, I knew nothing.

Apparently, Mary Anne lived entirely off rabbits. Whenever she needed anything, she would give a rabbit in exchange. And if one of her neighbours wanted a rabbit, they'd take her a jug of milk or something else in exchange. I used to smile when Trevor Jones smiled over Mary Anne and the rabbits. I pictured her busy most of her day, tending a long row of home-made rabbit hutches.

Trading and bartering seems to have been one of the main ways people got by on Sodom. Lewis Jones' great-grandfather had had 'a string of donkeys' and made his living by cutting down elder trees and carrying them on his donkeys to Holywell, ten miles or so away. He sold the elder to the local clog makers for only a few pennies.

Elder is plentiful in Wales. From the clog makers he went on down to the shore of the Dee estuary just below Holywell, where he gathered cockles and mussels which he sold on his return trip. It was an ingenious system of trading two items that he gathered for free.

Trevor Jones, Bryn Ffynnon, said that his grandfather made a few pennies from trapping foxes, alive and uninjured, and carrying them in a sack on his back eight miles to the headquarters of the local foxhunt. Catching a wild fox alive is no easy feat, as foxes are more canny and shy than almost any other wild animal. Trevor's family lived in a tiny house, now completely disappeared, known as Twll y Mwg (the smokehole).

'And that was all it was – just a little Twll y Mwg. Good Laws, yes! How they lived then!' Trevor would say, shaking his head and smiling.

Twll y Mwg was so small and hidden away in a copse that it was never entered on any of the detailed maps of the area. These old men knew almost all that could be known of the hillside. A place like Sodom had no written records. Lewis Jones remembers that his family owned a field in Sodom, 'but the case with deeds was lost and no one could remember which field it was and so it was lost'. How the family could themselves have forgotten which field they mowed and farmed is hard to imagine. The truth was that they probably had never tended this field, they were too busy elsewhere. Nothing was normal in Sodom, nothing was quite as it seemed.

A lot happened at night. Trevor Jones, Bryn Ffynnon, recounted, 'If you were coming home late at night, you'd meet plenty of people coming and going. One'd be just taking his donkeys out to feed on the sides of the road. Another fellow would be bringing up a load of cut grass from the railway.

You'd stop and have a chat. There was always plenty of comings and goings at night. Some of them just taking the donkeys out to feed.'

When Trevor Jones told me that everyone was on the move at night, it made a faint echo in my mind. At night? Why at night? There was a simple explanation – the donkeys were grazing other people's grass but, if everyone was out, there couldn't be too many secrets! I had a talent for letting strange pieces of information pass me by.

Almost everything that moved in Sodom – that wasn't moved by manpower – was moved by donkeys. These donkeys didn't belong to the people who lived in Sodom; they belonged to the men who gave donkey rides along the nearby seafront at Rhyl all summer. At the end of the summer the donkey owners looked for cheap pasture and keep for their animals over the winter. People in Sodom offered such good rates that many of the donkeys ended up spending the winter there.

The terms were good for a reason. One man, who 'took donkeys from Rhyl', had them working harder in winter than in summer, according to Lewis Jones. This man travelled around on top of one of the donkeys – but one day he went too far. He tried to make the donkey carry him and a large load of coal up the hill to Sodom. The donkey had barely started up the first hill from the railway station before it sank to its knees and lay down. The donkey's indignant rider scrambled to his feet amongst all the coal and tried to make the donkey get up, but it just lay there as if it had lost interest in life. Eventually, the man went back to the station to get the porter to help him get the donkey to its feet. Will, the porter in Bodfari at that time, came slowly up the hill, but when he got to the donkey he bent down and said in a stage whisper, 'If I were you, I wouldn't get up either,' and he walked back down the hill.

Since donkeys were thought of as an asset, and not a liability, some of the poorest and most improvident people of Sodom ended up with the most donkeys. And so, summer and winter, one of the occupations for the people of Sodom with no land whatsoever was finding free forage for their donkeys. People volunteered to cut Bodfari graveyard, 'plenty of good grass there!', the embankments of the railway, the roadsides, or wherever. And if you didn't have any place to cut, you took your donkeys out at night to look for feed. Some people just let their donkeys loose to forage wherever they could.

Sodom seems to have lacked any conventional organization but for one woman, Betsy Lewis, who occupied a role almost unique for a woman at that time, she was the deacon of the Baptist chapel at Sodom.

The chapel is a tiny building, only fourteen feet by sixteen feet inside. It accommodated a few rows of seats arranged like theatre bleachers, rising towards the back. It is the only public

Meyriel Edge

In the 1840s the Methodist Connection became alarmed at what they saw as 'the ignorance and sheer paganism' of this area. The Calvinists built a small chapel to be called Capel Salem, but they soon departed, and the place became known as just Sodom Chapel.

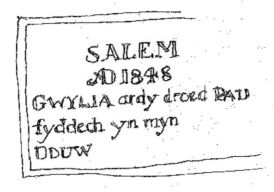

building there ever was in Sodom, which had no shops, not even an inn. It was built in 1848, long before Tremeirchion or neighbouring Bodfari had their own purpose-built chapels.

In fact, the Baptists had a very old secret meeting place in Sodom, dating back long before the freedom of religion was established in Britain. The farm where the religious meetings were held is still called Bryn Ffynnon (Hill of the Well) – the well was used to baptize the congregation.

The only indication that Capel Salem, Sodom's chapel, was indeed a chapel was a small exhortation in Welsh that was inscribed in a tablet above the door, 'Go carefully when you visit the house of God'.

The quotation from Ecclesiastes seems to have been chosen with the reputation of this community in mind. The people of the area were far from docile and taciturn, even when they all collected there each Sunday as they apparently did for nearly a century. The tiny chapel must have been a bit like a box of unstable explosives. That the chapel functioned more or less like other chapels was entirely due to the stocky Betsy Lewis. She tried, summer and winter, to keep the congregation of the chapel on a peaceful law-abiding track. 'Everyone had to behave!' Trevor, Bryn Ffynnon, told me with a grin. In spite of all her efforts, she seems to have been successful only when she met her neighbours eye-to-eye in the narrow confines of that tiny hillside chapel.

10

The declamations of Margaret Edwards

CRAZINESS WAS SO common in Sodom that it became part of the way of life. Did the wild hillsides draw people who didn't fit in down in the valley, or did the deprivation and isolation of Sodom turn people's minds? Or was it just that these people, the children and grandchildren of others who had 'run' to Sodom, had inherited some of the waywardness of their ancestors? For whatever reason madness, ranging from private obsession to conspicuous lunacy, could be found at nearly every house.

Jenny Pritchard of Plesyn refused to listen to the radio during the Second World War because she didn't want the Germans to be able to eavesdrop on her in her kitchen. Her craziness was more of a chronic pre-industrial innocence, but Margaret Edwards was a different story. She lived in Sodom for nearly seventy years, mad for a good part of that time, but tolerated by and even on good terms with most of her neighbours.

Margaret Edwards became the best-known inhabitant of Sodom. She was the only hill dweller that everyone from the village and valley was prepared to talk about, and she was well known for good reason. Margaret Edwards lived at Bryn Gwilym which, like most Welsh names, is logical and

Bryn Gwilym

Meyriel Edge

Bryn Gwilym perches on a ledge on the steepest climb of all in Sodom.

descriptive. It stands at the head of the Gwilym stream valley, and that was probably the main reason why Bryn Gwilym was unique.

The house perches on a tiny flattened area on one of the steepest banks on the whole escarpment. The road past Bryn Gwilym is so steep that I remember having to back down to take a second run at the hill. Hard to imagine how a horse and cart would ever get up it. Below Bryn Gwilym the land drops swiftly down to the fields around Nantgwilym Uchaf and, from there on, more gently to the road from Tremeirchion to Bodfari.

This scoop in the land creates a natural amphitheatre. Whatever noise is made in front of Bryn Gwilym carries down to the valley below as if it was amplified. Right up to the time that I moved into the cottage down the slope from Bryn Gwilym, the house was occupied by the last of the 'old-timers', Tom Jones, who lived alone – but not in complete seclusion.

When Tom started his motorbike, it sounded like a small airplane taking off. When he cut wood, it sounded like someone demolishing the house. Most people would be embarrassed at having their daily activities broadcast to the valley, and Tom probably didn't bless this feature of his house, but in her day Margaret Edwards made the most of this natural forum.

Margaret Edwards was a big woman, around six feet tall and, as if to dramatize her height, she dressed from head to foot in white, 'always spotless and clean'. White is an odd colour for a countrywoman to wear, and an ironic one considering her sanity, or lack of it, but she wore it probably for a good purpose. For Margaret Edwards is best remembered standing on the little terrace in front of Bryn Gwilym, beating an old metal lid against a tree. Standing on the steep slope dressed in white, she could be seen from half a mile away. Everyone knew what would happen next. After a few moments of this beating, she would start to shout with a voice that rang out loud and clear.

Some men cutting hay in a field near Bryn Gwilym one day were unprepared for Margaret Edwards, and when she appeared in white and started to declaim, they 'dropped their scythes and ran'.

Clothed in white, like an ancient Druid, Margaret Edwards shouted down towards the valley, cursing her enemies. She may have been responsible for the fact that no one from the village visited Sodom casually to collect blackberries, hazelnuts or mushrooms – the three wild harvests that grow abundantly on the hillslopes and which are, by law, for anyone to take.

But just because few people passed on the steep road

Michael Newbold

The view from Sodom down over the valley on a winter's day. A powerful nor'easter is driving the smoke from the cottage where I lived while researching this book.

leading past Bryn Gwilym didn't mean that Margaret Edwards lacked an audience. On the contrary, my Uncle Phillip told me, 'You'd be coming along the bottom road [the road between Tremeirchion and Bodfari] and you'd find a crowd of people standing in the road by Nant Gwilym. They'd just be standing there, listening to Margaret Edwards shouting from Bryn Gwilym.'

Clearly, Margaret had a powerful voice because, even with the peculiar acoustics of her hillside house, the distance from Bryn Gwilym to the bottom road was over a quarter of a mile and over that distance you could hear not only her shouting but just what she was saying.

One of the people Margaret Edwards had most to say about was the man who lived at Nant Gwilym, the farm right below Bryn Gwilym. This was the farm that surrounded Nantlys, and it was let to Enos Jones until the late 1920s. Margaret Edwards had a particular dislike for Enos, and she started up a hailstorm of accusations against this farmer. I knew that there had been a serious rift between my family and Enos Jones, but no one ever explained why.

Margaret Edwards would start to shout, and Nant Gwilym would shout back. She said he'd been with other women. Enos Jones seemed to embody, for her, the fickleness of men from which she had herself suffered, either in fact or in her imagination. Margaret Edwards' husband died at Bryn Gwilym in 1912, but no one remembers him there.

Unfortunately for Enos, Margaret Edwards' unusual voice carried right down the mountain as far as his own back door. From her high vantage point she could even see when he entered and left his house, and who visited him. He must have dreaded hearing the tin lid start to beat. It was, in all probability, Enos Jones who started a campaign of his own against his vociferous neighbour.

The trouble with Margaret Edwards' shouting was that it wasn't all crazy and that's what upset people the most – it was wild, it was rude and crude, but there was enough truth in it to make good listening if you didn't feel too vulnerable.

Her worst nightmare, and possibly the reason for her madness, was the death of most of her children. 'She used to shout that she'd buried her babies in the country all around,' Trevor Jones, Bryn Ffynnon, told me. Four of her six children died before the age of ten, but three of them at least were buried in Tremeirchion churchyard. According to one neighbour, Margaret Edwards wasn't always mad, but she'd had a mental relapse, connected with a mysterious young girl who lived with her in the early 1900s. Trevor Jones, Bryn Ffynnon, described the child as 'a beautiful young girl with long blonde hair'. No one knew exactly who she was. The girl disappeared one winter. She had apparently caught diphtheria, the dreaded disease of that time – and died.

Though the valley dwellers kept their distance from

Margaret Edwards, she was welcoming and hospitable enough to the inhabitants of Sodom. Dan Owen used to fight with his brother for the job of 'taking a hundredweight of coal from the station on a donkey. She'd give you a good tea and a penny.' At other times Dan Owen would cut the grass for her just for the tea alone. And that, apparently, was worth fighting for.

She entertained her neighbours, the Pendletons, who used to live at Nantgwilym Uchaf, for tea. She would make the tea and hand around pieces of a cake that she had made but then, when everyone was enjoying a moment of repose, she sometimes jumped up and started shouting,

'Listen! They're at it again!'

Margaret was shouting through the door into the parlour. Then she'd fling open the door and scream,

'Here! Have this! Just leave me alone!'

She'd hurl the plate, cake and all, into the dark room, but the voices were rarely satisfied. When this happened, the Pendletons would slip out quietly.

From 1890 onwards, Margaret Edwards had an increasing hatred of certain men, Enos Jones and then an English aristocrat called Lord Devonport, who she held responsible for some of her children's deaths.

While she was hitting the old lid against the tree, she started to shout that she was beating Lord Devonport, a wealthy grocer, who became the Minister of Food Control in the First World War.

'She said he was keeping food from the poor. There was a terrible shortage. They hadn't organized things right. They were more careful in the Second World War,' my Uncle Phillip explained.

Margaret Edwards was not just a soapbox orator, shouting against the invisible politician two hundred miles away in London. On the horizon, looking out from Bryn Gwilym, on the heather-clad expanse of the Denbigh Moors, Lord and

Lady Devonport had built a shooting lodge. It was no simple summer house, but a huge square house, almost as big as Nantlys.

According to my mother, Lady Devonport chose the site during a shooting party one balmy hot August day around 1908 and never returned until the house had been fully furnished in November 1914. Lady Devonport climbed out of her carriage and suddenly felt the cold moorland wind which sweeps across this high ground almost uninterrupted from the Irish Sea. She expressed disgust at such a wretched climate and the exposed situation of the new house, climbed back into her carriage and ordered the coachman to leave immediately. My mother told me the house was never occupied by the Devonport family, but Lord Devonport later wrote that they spent several Edwardian and post-war shooting seasons there before abandoning the house a few decades after it was built.

The ruins of the house now stand like a prop for a Victorian thriller – a huge house on the top of a bleak moor. One day my family explored the house, and we were challenged on the way out by a farmer whose sheep now sheltered in the ruins. In some ways the house looked inhabited – rich red velvet curtains still hung in front of the floor-to-ceiling wooden windows, but the expensive wallpapers and velvet curtains were decaying from the wet wind that Lady Devonport had so despised.

And so Margaret Edwards was not quite so crazy shouting from one hilltop to the next. In her extreme poverty, she was outraged by a man who could afford to build a huge shooting lodge. The people of North Wales knew his new house would be empty for all but a few weeks of the year at the best of times. In the dark days of December 1916, when food from the outside world scarcely reached North Wales, they learned he was now the Minister of Food Control, in charge of feeding the whole of Britain.

Margaret Edwards' staged attacks on Lord Devonport

probably sealed her fate. Complaints about her 'bizarre behaviour' were received by the police and a small posse was sent up to Bryn Gwilym in October 1918. From her sharp vantage point, Margaret Edwards saw them coming. 'She went in and locked the door with furniture behind it,' Trevor Bryn Ffynnon told me. When the police arrived, they were confronted with a torrent of verbal abuse from behind the barricaded door. She threatened to cut her own throat and that of the child with her, according to the official hospital report. The police finally broke in through the rear and captured Margaret Edwards. There was no child. Was she just a phantom of the girl with blonde hair?

Margaret Edwards was carried down to the North Wales Counties Mental Hospital across the valley. According to Trevor Jones, Bluebell, the inhabitants of this asylum were not restricted to people who were a hazard to themselves or society. 'They took anyone who was a bit odd, unusual – they were stricter then!' As a result many of the inmates were gifted. 'They had a fine orchestra. It played at a lot of places. There was plenty of talent,' Trevor Bluebell assured me.

I hoped that when I uncovered the record of Margaret Edwards at the North Wales Counties Mental Hospital there would have been a happier ending. Instead, the notes were brief and lacking in any warmth. She was diagnosed as having 'delusional insanity with oral hallucinations' – the voices. She was seventy years old, but even at this advanced age Margaret didn't calm down; if anything, she became wilder away from Sodom. One doctor wrote she was 'bad-tempered, abusive, language disgusting. She foamed and raved.'

In the absence of her neighbours in Sodom and in the valley, Margaret Edwards found new causes to fight for, including a problem in which she accused people of saying that she hadn't paid for her clothes and shoes. Margaret Edwards died at the age of seventy-nine, almost ten years after her initial confinement.

In its annual report that year, the North Wales Counties Mental Hospital boasted that it no longer used physical restraints on the patients. Nevertheless, it attributed the insanity of some twenty-eight per cent of the patients to the moon – the old lunacy.

11

A bit of a witch

WOMEN SEEMED TO be the leaders on the mountain. Whether it was the cleverest, the craziest, the most eccentric, the most law-abiding or the most mysterious of all the inhabitants of Sodom, the answer in every case was a woman.

The most notorious inhabitant of Sodom was Miriam Crewe. Many people who lived in the village refused to discuss her. Some froze at the mention of her name and then said that they had never heard of her. Nearly everyone who lived in the valley, when I moved back into one of the hillslope cottages, seemed to feel that the least said the better.

Only my family and the old men of Sodom – loners, bachelors and widowers – were prepared to admit they knew anything. Even then they were unwilling to do much more than repeat her name, 'Miriam, yes – Mirr-ee-aam Crewe'. They pronounced each vowel with special emphasis in the Welsh way – dwelling on the name as if that said it all, then they'd settle back in their chairs again with a smile and say no more. Whenever I talked to these men, I'd mention her name and they would almost always veer off the subject again. At the end of it all, even to the people who knew her, Miriam seems to have been a mystery, which is just what she wanted.

Miriam Crewe was born and lived all her life at Bryn

Caredig, a long low cottage consisting of just two rooms ten feet square apiece. Each of these rooms had its own front door, because this small cottage used to be two even smaller cottages – one room apiece – known as Bryn Caredig and Nant Caredig. Caredig means pleasant, which is ironic because under Miriam it came to have a very different connotation, and it still affected the people who passed there and grew up on the hill.

This was the house which made John Lidford giggle and laugh his special high-pitched cackle as he rode by with my sister and me on our ponies. His musical laugh would have played well on the stage. In fact, we never went by without stopping. John's aunt lived there when I was young and kept her pigs in the chapel, which was then referred to as Capel y Mochyn or 'chapel of the pig'. It became a local joke that in Sodom the pigs lived in the chapel, which was one more proof of the topsy-turviness of this hillside. John's aunt was tough, and she had to be, because anyone who lived in Miriam's old house risked acquiring her aura.

Miriam's mother lived at Nant Caredig when Miriam was born in 1863, the eldest of two girls. Miriam was christened on 6 April 1864, when the curate of Bodfari presented her with a little black leather-bound prayerbook. It was the practice in Bodfari to give the poorest parishioners a prayerbook at their christening. The Crewes must have lived at the edge of starvation, because they were one of only a dozen families or so who received poor aid from the church.

Curiously, though they had no money, the Crewes owned the two tiny cottages because the Caredigs were squatter cottages or 'tai unnos' (literally 'one-night houses'). By ancient custom, in Wales anyone could claim a house on common land if they could build themselves a turf or stone house during a single night and have smoke coming out of the chimney by dawn the following day. In many areas they also got as much land as they could cover by throwing an axe from the threshold of their new front door.

Bryn Caredig

Meynel Edge

Miriam Crewe made the Caredig cottages one of the most feared or respected places in Sodom, depending on who you talked to.

At Bryn Caredig it seems the axe travelled over twenty feet to the road in front of the house and even beyond. This little smallholding had, until very recently, always flowed out over the road, with all sorts of domestic and farm animals using the road as a comfortable dry place on which to lie. In the past many an animal wandered off down the road from Bryn Caredig, looking for better pastures. It was Miriam Crewe's pigs who stole Trevor Bryn Ffynnon's school lunch.

The Crewes lived at Bryn Caredig before the chapel was built, and either gave or sold the small plot of land on which it sits. Miriam's mother was probably one of the prime movers in the construction of the new chapel, which was one of the earliest Non-conformist chapels to be built in this area. In matters of religion, the hill people often led the valley. They had strong beliefs, even if people in the valley sometimes wondered which religion they were really loyal to. There were even rumours of paganism. I was curious to know if the old pantheism of the Celts and the Druids had lingered on the hilltops – it was one of the reasons why the hilltops fascinated me.

Miriam Crewe's first and probably only job was at the newly-built hall, far below in the valley, where she worked as a seamstress in the laundry room for my great-grandmother. She had the reputation of being 'a *good* cook', but she put herself down as just a seamstress in the census of 1881 – one of the few places where Miriam Crewe's name remains on record.

She must have worked well because she was always seen in a different light by my family, who disbelieved the rumours that were later spread about her. My aunt described her as a wise woman, but while she was working at Nantlys, Miriam Crewe entered into what was to be her real vocation.

She started telling fortunes by 'reading the tea'. Reading fortunes from teacups was a common method of fortune-telling amongst women in rural Wales. It was practised by almost every woman in Sodom, which was known for its fortune-tellers.

The fortune-teller would brew a pot of tea with care. As she poured the first cup for her client, some of the loose tea leaves from which the tea had been brewed would slip down the spout. The fortune-teller and her client would drink their tea quietly, right down to the dregs. Then the fortune-teller was ready to begin.

The client swirled her cup around and threw the last of her tea onto the floor or fire. The formation of the leaves that remained on the side of the cup, their quantity and type, gave the fortune-teller the only clues to the fortune which she then read. Unlike cards there was no clear one-to-one explanation of what a person would see in the cup.

I met one woman in Tremeirchion who admitted to being able to 'read the tea', but she had stopped long ago after seeing 'an evil-looking shape on the side of the cup'. Her name was Sarah Parry.

'It was like a man but with his arms raised over his head and all curled forwards. It was terrible. I was really afraid.'

Two days later her client found a man lying dead in the road in the same contorted position. This fortune-teller refused to 'read the tea' again. An optimist by nature, she didn't want to dabble in anything to do with death. She used to dismiss fortune-telling.

'There's nothing to it, you know. It's just a game. I learned it just for a laugh.'

There are many stories of women swearing off reading the cups in Sodom. One story is attributed to two different fortune-tellers who lived in Sodom. A mother and daughter came one day and begged to have their teacups read. The woman who was to read the cups didn't want to do it, but the visitors persuaded her – they had travelled a long way and the daughter was going to be married. The fortune-teller gave in. First she read the mother's cup and her fears subsided. There was nothing particular there. Then she turned to the daughter's cup and saw the worst. 'I can't read any further,' she said flatly. Three weeks later the girl died. That fortune-teller never 'read the cups' again.

But Miriam Crewe started to 'read the tea' and never stopped. With her apparent success at seeing into a person's past and predicting the future, her reputation grew. Many of the employees at Nantlys began to consult her. Around 1890 Miriam Crewe stopped working at Nantlys and gave birth to a baby boy, whom she named Tom. Miriam's mother was still alive, though very old, but because Miriam Crewe was unmarried her mother claimed the baby, who was referred to from then on as Miriam's baby brother. Miriam returned back to Bryn Caredig and hardly, if ever, descended into the valley again. But that did not stop her close relations with the people who worked at Nantlys. People were always coming and going up the lane. They'd take little parcels of food to get their fortunes read.

One day one of my uncles was taken up to Bryn Caredig, while the nursery maid went in to call on Miriam. He remembers catching a glimpse of Miriam at the door, 'a woman all in black but for a little lace collar and a white lace cap'.

While many valley dwellers wouldn't go past the mad Margaret Edwards' house, it is ironic that my uncle was taken right up to Bryn Caredig and saw the shadowy Miriam. Because of the closeness of Nantlys to Sodom, our family came to know Sodom better than many people from the village did. It was a strange relationship between wealth and poverty. But there was even more to it. My family, with enough eccentricities of their own, seemed to relish the people of the mountain and were certainly less disapproving than many people in the village. There was a practical side to it too. Nearly everyone in Sodom turned to my family at some time or another for help or advice, and we turned to them as well.

Reading the tea was not unusual, but the reputation that Miriam developed at reading the tea was. She was soon said to be someone with gifts. People who read the tea and were regarded as having gifts had plenty of visitors, including people in a crisis, who would travel a long distance to have their fortune told.

But it didn't stop there with Miriam. Some of her neighbours and customers believed that she did in fact 'have powers', the ability to influence events – in other words, witchcraft. One neighbour referred to Miriam as 'a bit of a witch'. Others called her a rogue and an impostor, and yet at the same time they remained afraid of her. On many a Sunday Betsy Lewis, the deacon who ran the chapel, denounced holding on to the wicked ungodly superstitions of the past, but some part of each person seems to have remained ill at ease about Miriam during her lifetime and long afterwards.

What worried her neighbours the most was the fact that Miriam wandered around the mountain at night with her donkeys. Even though this was a common practice in Sodom, it seems to have been different and infinitely more disliked when Miriam was 'abroad' at night. No one was sure what she was doing. If nothing else, 'she was taking her donkeys to feed at other people's haystacks'.

Miriam doesn't seem to have done anything to counteract her bad reputation. She didn't develop any close friendships with the other inhabitants of Sodom. She kept to herself after her mother died and had only one other companion apart from Tom, a woman by the name of Macmanners, who came to live at Bryn Caredig. Macmanners, as she was always referred to, was also deeply involved in fortune-telling and 'odd'. She was almost as shadowy and mysterious as Miriam herself, but, unlike Miriam, she was never accused of witchcraft.

Miriam Crewe had only one other friend, a tramp by the name of David Llwyd (Llwyd, which means grey in Welsh, was probably a nickname). David Llwyd used to stop off at Bryn Caredig on his way to and from Cartrefle, the workhouse in St Asaph.

Like many other tramps he crossed the ridge of the Clwydian Range by way of Tremeirchion and Sodom – which wasn't the shortest road, but it was the preferred route. The tramps seem to have felt almost at home in Sodom. David Llwyd certainly had a friend – he would always stop at Miriam Crewe's house 'for a good tea'. He might even have been the father of Tom.

Making the most of his ambiguous role between brother and son, Tom seems to have grown up independent of parental authority. Tom was at his worst at the one time when the people of Sodom were well behaved – in the chapel run by Betsy Lewis.

'Tom Crewe used to crawl under the staging where we were all sitting and once he put his hands up a woman's legs. She was there trying to kick him away, but she didn't like to say what was going on. So she was there trying to look like nothing was going on – but you could hear this rustling and stamping and shuffling and her getting redder all the time.

'Another time we were trying to go out after a service. The chapel was full of people. You couldn't move. They were all there trying to open the door. But the door wouldn't budge. Everyone tried and Betsy Lewis tried, but it wouldn't budge.

'Then someone looked out of the window and saw a wire running from the handle of the door to the gate onto the road. Tom had wired us in! Miriam Crewe had to climb out through the window and let them out,' Trevor smiled richly at the memory.

In the late summer of 1913, Miriam Crewe fell seriously ill and was admitted to the local sanatorium. She was accommodated in one of the free beds at the disposal of the Pennant family. Families who helped to finance the sanatorium were given beds that they could fill free of charge. All other patients had to pay seven pence a day. Miriam was too ill to notice that, at last, she was being waited upon by other people. She died a few weeks later at the age of only fifty-one. I could not discover the cause of her death – the hospital records only go back to the year after she died.

Eight months later, the First World War broke out. Tom Crewe volunteered and was soon transported to France. He was never seen again in Sodom. It was said that he survived the war, but decided not to return to Sodom.

Though she died before the First World War, in many ways Miriam Crewe never left the area. The people who knew her talked about her as though she was still listening. John Owen of Gwern Hwlkyn, a great storyteller in the 1930s, told everyone that two women haunted the lane in front of the chapel.

One night Trevor Jones, Bryn Ffynnon, was returning home up the road past the chapel on a dark, almost moonless night. Suddenly, just in front of Bryn Caredig, he saw a white shape, which was neither human nor animal, which hovered in the air. He stopped dead, unable to move, more frightened than he had ever been in his life. Then the shape slowly stretched forward. It was only the white marking on the face of a cow standing in the road, but Trevor Bryn Ffynnon said he never went that way at night again.

Considering the dearth of records about her, I was amazed to discover Miriam's prayerbook amongst Lizzie's things at Penuchaf. Miriam's prayerbook had in fact become Lizzie's prayerbook. Lizzie was given the prayerbook on Whitsunday 1939.

It is particularly odd, since bibles and prayerbooks have a special meaning in Wales where people used to have few possessions and religion formed an important part of most people's lives. A family Bible was often the only record of a family, with the dates of births and deaths all written down. A prayerbook was almost as important – people used the prayerbook of a dearly loved parent or grandparent. So how did Lizzie come to have and use the prayerbook of someone who was so distrusted?

The inscription which Lizzie wrote herself in the back of the prayerbook is even more ambiguous. In it she started to write 'The gift of Miriam Crewe', but then crossed out the Crewe and wrote Evans – the name of another woman in Sodom – and yet the book clearly had belonged to Miriam Crewe from the inscription in the front. Had Lizzie, as a child, developed a special friendship with Miriam, but was afraid to admit it or did Miriam Evans know something about Lizzie's line and think that this prayerbook would be good for her?

12

Herb beer

UP THE ROAD from Bryn Caredig, just above the lonely crossroads of Sodom, there still stands a small low house all by itself called Bryn Goleu, pronounced by Trevor Bryn Ffynnon as Brin Golly (the hilltop of light), which made him smile. He said it must have belonged to some English people once. Perched at the top of the slope, it is indeed on the brow of light. On clear evenings, long after the valley has fallen into darkness, Bryn Goleu is still bathed in the last gentle rays of the sun – extra light that helped no doubt on the evening when Bryn Goleu was built. Like Bryn Caredig, Bryn Goleu was put up in one night – built of slabs of turf by Lewis Jones' great-grandfather.

Because of its origins, Bryn Goleu never belonged to the Pennant estate. Instead, it belonged to nearly all of the families of Sodom who moved in and out of this small house in turn, as their fortunes rose and fell.

One of the most prolonged residents of Bryn Goleu was the family of Trevor Jones, Bryn Ffynnon, as he was called, after the farm just across the road from Bryn Goleu, where he lived later. Trevor Jones was the only man I ever met who felt no shyness about Sodom. He loved it for its wild history.

I first met Trevor on a windy winter's day in 1977 when I

Bryn Goleu, a house that was built by the family of Lewis Jones in one night. Once a tŷ unnos was erected, the owner could improve it with some stone after a year's occupation.

was driving back along the hilltop road from Penuchaf. This road came down past Bryn Goleu to the crossroads of Sodom. As I passed another abandoned cottage, I saw a new notice with big red letters on a freshly painted white sign: 'No Trespassers. Keep Out.' Instead of making me stay away, the sign made me slow down. Notices like that were rare in this area, particularly as this abandoned farm belonged to my father, who didn't hold with 'No Trespassing' signs. He believed that everyone should be allowed to walk through the countryside.

Immediately behind the heavily wired gate were two short, elderly men wrestling with a sheep. I had never seen either of them before. I stopped and, without thinking, started to walk towards them. The two men and I watched each other suspiciously. There is an old fear about approaching people in strange circumstances in desolate rural areas – you might find out more than is good for you. One of the men spoke first.

'Hellaaw!' he said slowly, with the characteristic Welsh pronunciation and emphasis on the last syllable. The strength of his intonation indicated that Welsh was his first and preferred language, at which I was inept.

'Hello.' I sounded all too English and wished I had stayed

in my car. The man who had spoken left the sheep to the other man and advanced to a few feet short of the barricaded and heavily wired gate.

I searched for something to say, 'This is a new sign, isn't it?'

'Oh, the sign,' he said, beginning to smile. 'I put it up the other day to stop people in their cars coming into the field to see the old house. Half the time they never close the gate, and then I have to go around looking for my sheep.'

I realized that he must be the neighbouring farmer who was renting the fields of Pant Glas, and he guessed that I was the daughter of the landlord of this farm. We had never met before.

To fill the ensuing silence I told him that I was trying to find out more about Lizzie Jones from Penuchaf and the people who used to live in Sodom. Almost instantly he dismantled his impressive barricade and slipped through the gate. I could see his face for the first time beneath the old cloth cap pulled down aslant over the corner of his face. Underneath was a good-looking man, with eyes lit up like a small child's. He looked fifty at most, but he was in fact nearly seventy the day we met.

'And where are you living now?' he asked with sharp curiosity.

'At Nantgwilym Uchaf.'

'Oh!' he said with a big grin. 'I'll drop down and see you then when I'm going by on my bike. I go past there nearly every day when I go to see the sheep.'

Though he still farmed up here, Trevor and his wife had moved down to the valley. The road past Nantgwilym Uchaf was not the most direct road for him, but he liked to see the whole of the slope – up one way and back down the other.

A week or so later Trevor appeared in front of Nantgwilym Uchaf with the same cap and another characteristic feature I came to know, an old canvas bag slung diagonally across his body to prevent him losing it on his bike. I was working in the garden. He looked a little bemused at the sight of one of the Pennants living and working like an inhabitant of Sodom. To cover his astonishment he started to talk rapidly about Sodom and barely paused for breath until I finally persuaded him to sit on a small wobbly child's bench that stood in front of the house. He did not want to go into the house.

If he was surprised, so was I. After all the evasions of other people I had talked to, here was someone telling me all about the old days of Sodom before I had even got out my notebook.

Why? I discovered that telling the old stories was Trevor's favourite pastime – he took it so seriously it was like a vocation. I came to know the way he told his tales. He would settle down on a stone wall or stand, with one foot propped up against a fence or on a stone, and start running through names, throwing out brief comments about each one – always mentioning Miriam Crewe with a particular soft chuckle. I wondered how to stop him or slow him down. Then I learned he was a performer, reciting his repertoire. The listener had to choose one of the many stories he mentioned, catch him with a question, and then he would start to talk, sometimes staying just with that person, but more often wandering to and fro, talking about other people before finally returning to the main subject.

Some anecdotes he repeated time and again, but it was more like a chant or the retelling of a favourite saga than the mere repetition of information.

By the end of his first visit, Sodom had changed for me. It had changed from a place of puzzling shadows to a bustling community with tales more curious than I had ever guessed at. But, as it turned out, he hadn't even told me the most important story.

One of the stories he told me on this and many other future occasions concerned his own family. Trevor was the only person in the whole of Sodom and Tremeirchion who was prepared to tell not only the stories of the community, but also the story of his own family. He referred often, but only in passing, to his grandfather who had lived at the tiny house called Twll y Mwg, and who had carried live foxes to the hunt on his back.

As a young boy he had walked with the other children from Sodom to and fro from the school in Tremeirchion, which meant passing through the animals that collected on the road in front of Miriam Crewe's house. He scampered past the pigs that chased them for their lunch, and donkeys that sometimes followed them to school.

But, as a boy, he had learned about something that few men in Wales ever knew about unless they practised the art themselves. He had learnt about 'the herbs'.

Herbal remedies were made throughout Sodom. Bunches of dark green desiccated leaves hung from the low rafters in almost every kitchen up to the Second World War. Women used these herbs not only for teas and tonics, but ground them up and used fat or soap to make ointments, or boiled them to make certain decoctions to treat their own families and animals.

Miriam Crewe probably dabbled in cures. When Trevor was thinking about that he exclaimed, with unusual fierceness, 'There were an awful lot of quacks then. Umpteen women died.' Presumably in childbirth. But Trevor's mother developed a special reputation for cures. According to one of her neighbours she was a 'clever woman, always making cures'. Making herbal remedies dominated her life.

Trevor Jones said that when there was someone very ill in Sodom, his mother became obsessed.

'She'd be up all night worrying out a cure. She even cured diphtheria. One family had two children with diphtheria. The neighbours wouldn't even stop at the gate. No one would go near them. Diphtheria was bad then. Everyone was scared. But she went in and she kept making things for them and they got better. The district nurse was shocked.

'A lot of people died then. One boy had appendicitis. They

operated on him at the farm. He died. When my brother got pneumonia with pleurisy, the district nurse said it was all over with him. He was as white as a sheet, lying there doing nothing. But she stayed up all night for two weeks and in the end he became alright again.'

Mrs Jones enjoyed a curious love-hate relationship with this district nurse, who was the only representative of orthodox medicine who visited Sodom. No one could pay for the doctor, who called on patients in Tremeirchion. The district nurse plainly wished that Mrs Jones would mind her own business and leave medicine to the experts, but over the years she grudgingly came to respect her. She even became one of Mrs Jones' best customers for what Trevor's mother was most famous for – her herb beer.

Meyriel Edge

The ingredients Mrs Jones used for her herb beer grew along the roadsides. In the background is the outline of Moel-y-Gaer, an Iron Age hill fort.

Most herbalists would work alone, growing herbs and collecting them in the wild, drying or brewing them up fresh, never telling a soul what they were up to. But Mrs Jones was so busy in May collecting ingredients for her herb beer that she had to ask her children – including Trevor – to help. When they were just right she sent her children out.

In May the roadsides and hedgerows around were a riot of lush green growth. From amongst these Trevor Jones, Bryn Ffynnon, picked out certain herbs, dandelions, wild carrot, nettles, and particularly the strange plant with long yellow spiky flowers, agrimony.

In the sixteenth and seventeenth centuries agrimony was a panacea for almost every ailment. It fell into disuse by other herbalists, but in Mrs Jones' herb beer it was a key ingredient, and the readiness of agrimony deciding when the beer would be made. When all the herbs had been collected,

'She boiled them up in a huge copper and then put them in a big pan with brewer's yeast and waited for a day or two and then poured it into jars and bottles.'

The bottles didn't always survive. It was hard to judge when fermentation had subsided enough for the brew to be ready for bottling, particularly if you were aiming for a fizzy brew. Mrs Jones didn't always time it right and she even used screw-top bottles, which were much riskier than corks which pop-out to release excess pressure.

'There used to be explosions in the middle of the night – bottles just going off,' Trevor chuckled.

No one will say why Mrs Jones' herb beer was so popular – because of its curative properties or its strong alcoholic content? Whatever the reason, the brewing and selling of herb beer was probably the largest legitimate industry in Sodom.

The Jones' family life was not quite so organized and business-like. According to Trevor, his father came back one day and found a tramp in the house.

'The tramps who came through used to go into houses

sometimes and take things, but this one wasn't after money, he was after women.

'Well, when he came back and found him there, he threw the tramp out into the road just like he was, wearing almost nothing at all. And threw everything after him – clothes, stud boxes, nails and anything else he could find.'

Possibly, as a result of this episode, John Jones decided he needed a change of scene. According to one of his neighbours,

'He was driving his trap one day when he decided to go to Canada. So he stopped the pony and got out of the trap just where he was and walked off to the station. No one saw or heard of him again for a year or two when he suddenly turned up again. He made a lot of money there, too.'

Everyone seems to have believed that John Jones struck it rich. Is this what he told them? Another man from Sodom said he'd been working in the stock exchange and made a lot of money. 'He went to and fro, coming back when the exchange was good.'

There was a misunderstanding of John Jones' mysterious travels on many levels.

During one of his return trips John Jones constructed a shed from rough wooden uprights, covered all around and on top with corrugated iron which became known as Pen-y-Ffridd Zinc.

I have looked over the gate at this building. It would have made uncomfortable accommodation even for an animal, but, according to Trevor, his family was obliged to move there for a time. Even then, they couldn't afford to pay the rent, but John Jones, on a subsequent return visit, paid his arrears and made his name in the area as a rich man. The affairs of the family improved somewhat and they were able to move back into Bryn Goleu. Then John Jones' trips away grew longer – and Mrs Jones fell victim to her own skill in brewing.

'It was the herb beer that made her go to drink. She

went off to market and came back drunk as a lord,' John Dyke commented. He was standing by the open door of the Dinorben (the pub in Bodfari) one Wednesday evening when he saw Mrs Jones going up the hill with all her bags. The hill going up past Bodfari church was a steep one.

'I didn't see how she was going to make it. She just got around the corner when there was a terrible noise and all the cans came rolling around the corner down the hill with Mrs Jones rolling after them.'

When Mrs Jones died, all her recipes, including the one for her very popular herb beer, died with her. Mr Dyke commented on the passing of all the old recipes.

'Gone west. All gone west. The old folk, they'd never tell you anything – just, d'you like it? They wouldn't even tell their own daughter.'

There was a belief among many herbalists that secrecy was important – perhaps it was just preserving the uniqueness of their preparations, perhaps it might make their cure seem even more special, more powerful if the patient didn't know that it was just a sprig of rosemary boiled in buttermilk.

But more than that, it seems to have been a ritual, a belief like that of the ancient Druids that things should not be written down, that the mystery around her recipes that may have changed from year to year helped in the cure. What mattered was the way in which a cure was prepared, the attitude, the manner was as important in helping to bring about a healing.

Trevor Jones, Bryn Ffynnon, remembered his mother working at night under 'an awful old light', probably a paraffin lamp with its glass clouded with condensation and dust. She would be fussing, worrying and brewing when there was no one else around.

Mrs Jones was a real herbalist, instead of just following recipes. She was continually trying to find new ones and, through self-dosing, find out which of the available herbs in Sodom could cure or speed the recovery of a specific illness.

Her dedication may in fact have done her patients more good than the doctors from the nearby towns, whose costliness meant that hill dwellers never called them until someone was at death's door. But Mrs Jones, in her rough hilltop clothing, was quickly there and – paid or unpaid – set to work.

meat. Rabbits were big business and over and over again landlords hung on not only to the rights to the game, but also to the rabbits.

Even my great-grandfather, who was usually generous towards his tenants, had a standard clause in all his rental agreements, which read as follows:

All game, fish, wildfowl *and rabbits* [my emphasis], are reserved to the landlord with full and free liberty for him or his licensees, or for his or their friends and servants to shoot on the premises at pleasure.

The issue of who was entitled to catch rabbits wasn't just a local problem – it was nationwide and became so controversial that it was discussed many times in parliament. Finally, in 1880, an act entitled the Ground Game Act, which concerned itself almost entirely with rabbits, was passed. It was intended to resolve this problem by giving every tenant farmer the absolute right to catch rabbits on his own land by day. (Rabbits used to stay in their burrows most of the day and only went out to feed as it began to get dark.) To protect farmers from unfair pressure from their landlords, the act further stated that a tenant farmer could never sell or give away this right absolutely.

This act, which should have been revolutionary in places like Tremeirchion and Sodom, had no effect at all. Landowners, tenants, poachers and keepers all talk even now as if the act had never existed, let alone been in force for over a hundred years. After the act passed, tenant farmers, instead of catching rabbits by day as they were now allowed to do, still went out by night, thereby breaking the law.

Things continued exactly as before. Did no one ever hear about their new rights? Or did the keepers strenuous efforts make sure that people felt nothing had changed? Or was it that catching rabbits by night was just the way it was done, law or no law? Most farmers in fact wouldn't have had time to use valuable daylight hours netting the odd daytime rabbit.

The keepers were the people who stood to lose the most by the Ground Game Act because rabbits weren't prized by landowners, but most keepers substantially increased their own low incomes by 'controlling the rabbits'.

John Roberts, a farmer from West Wales, testified before the Royal Commission in 1894 that:

> Although I have a right to the rabbits, yet I fear the consequence of making use of my rights. I have arranged with a man to catch rabbits on a certain portion of my farm, but in the meantime Lord Harlech's keepers appeared and commenced ferreting wholesale. When I remonstrated, I received a threatening letter from Lord Harlech, intimating that if I interfered with them he would see my landlord about it.

The night after he testified the same keepers approached Mr Roberts and claimed that, for one pound, he had given them the exclusive right to catch rabbits over his land for a year. When this bargain was described at the hearing the following day, someone in the room pointed out that this sale was not only after the fact, but also contrary to the terms of the Ground Game Act. Lawyers for the other side claimed that the transaction wasn't illegal, but merely void, and yet they continued to flourish the farmer's receipt in court.

What was law and what was accepted in this medieval business of who owned and was entitled to take the wild animals and birds of the countryside? These were apparently two separate things. Owning game was a subject that tended to bring out the worst of English snobbery. No wonder the people in Tremeirchion and Sodom were confused over their rights to rabbits.

The Ground Game Act wasn't any use to most of the people in Sodom because most of them only rented a field or two at most, and the rabbits had long since left the vicinity of these zealous rabbit catchers for the wide open spaces of the neighbouring estates. The slopes of Sodom, which

142

belonged to my family and one other landowner, was just such a place. Rabbits thrived, digging their burrows in the soft, sandy soil. The area became so abundant with rabbits that the whole north-eastern slope was and still is called The Warren because of the hundreds, even thousands, of rabbit holes that honeycombed the hillslope. By 1900 the whole slope was crisscrossed with enough wire to trip any poacher, and patrolled every night by keepers who farmed the rabbits commercially. Perhaps it was these rabbit-infested slopes that led to the curious development of Sodom.

Near the end of the time that I lived at Nantgwilym Uchaf in 1977, I wrote an article about Sodom for a local newspaper. In the article I used many of the anecdotes Trevor Jones, Bryn Ffynnon, had told me, including one candid one about his mother. I wondered how he would feel seeing it all in print. Would he regret his openness? I left for America very soon after the article came out and didn't manage to call in on him as I had wanted to do. It was a year before I returned to Wales again. As soon as I did, I went to see Trevor – this time not to ask questions, but just to say hello.

When he saw me at the door, I could see immediately that something had changed. He didn't greet me with his old familiar grin. He silently turned around and walked into a small back room which was dark even though it was day, because the curtains were tightly drawn. The only light was a small lamp near a table covered in a dark brown rug-like cloth. Trevor sat down at the table. I was confused and apprehensive – was he so angry he could barely say a word?

Then he started to talk – not in his former playful way, skipping from one subject to the next, but this time with seriousness and urgency. He barely paused again for more than an hour. With an uncanny memory he remembered all his previous omissions. This time he told me the other half of the story – more about which herbs his mother had used and her secret brewing at night. But more than anything else, he told me about what happened at night, and what they had caught.

I saw that he had made up his mind that he wanted me to know more than just the funny stories about the crazy characters like Miriam Crewe and Margaret Edwards. If I was going to write about Sodom, I had to write about what happened at night. He began,

'You can't do anything on a night with a moon. The keepers can see you a quarter of a mile off in the moonlight, and you need wind. Rabbits have got wonderful noses, but they're no good in a wind. You need a dark night with enough wind. You have to go around them [the rabbits], not making any noise and keep the wind always coming from behind them, always coming from behind the rabbits.'

He waved his arms around to imitate a good steady wind. We were both back there now on a moonless night with the wind blowing.

'If it shifts, one gust from you to the rabbits, they'll be quarter of a mile off and still running. As long as you keep the wind coming towards you and it's strong, it'll even carry your footsteps away. When the wind is coming towards you, you can get right up close, and you need that if you're working with the nets.

'We were the first people to bring in long nets. They'd never been used around here before. The people of Sodom were better at catching rabbits than anyone else for miles!'

I asked how did the nets work?

'There's four hundred feet of net to one of the new nets. You tighten the wire, top and bottom to get plenty of slack and then you have to know the runs [the pathways down which the rabbits bolt when frightened].

'If you don't know the runs, you'll be going around all night for nothing. We used to set the net across a run when the rabbits were out eating – early evening just after dark was best – then one or two would go around the back to frighten them. You could make enough money in one night to live for a month.

'You can catch anything in a long net. I fell into one one night and had a job getting out. When I saw Old Royals a bit later he was saying "Duw, there's been a badger in my net." He had a big hole. We had fun then.

'Mary Anne, Pwll y Carw, lived on nothing but catching rabbits. We used to boil them and wrap them in bacon and have roast rabbit. That was worth eating! Pigeons too. You could shoot one in March and set it up nicely in a patch of turnips as if it was alive and get dozens. We got hares as well. Ate jugged hare.'

That made me smile. While rabbits were considered 'poor food' and rarely served in the big houses, hares were a prized delicacy, especially when 'jugged' or cooked in port and redcurrant jelly, a rare favourite in our house, always cooked up by my aunt.

'We ate nightjar too – they make a strange noise at night just in the spring – that's how you could find them. And partridges too. Good Laws, yes! They're small but they're fierce. They'll fight a cat. You need a silk net to get them. We'd set up snares in a field of new stubble. As soon as we heard a commotion, we'd throw the net over. There were keepers who'd put thorns out in their fields just to tear the nets.

'Some poachers didn't even go into the woods – got their pheasants in the open. There was a keeper who was rearing pheasants down in St Asaph – he lost them all one night to a good poacher. Another man sneaked up to the pens of young pheasants they were rearing at Bryngwyn Hall – while the keepers were having a nap. He put them all in a sack and took them down to Pontruffydd [another big house three miles in the other direction] and sold the lot. Those days there were no police about!

'One keeper left a straw dummy all dressed up in his hut and went off drinking. It fooled us for a minute, but it didn't take us long to find out! It was dangerous as well. One lot of poachers shot a gamekeeper in the legs. It was bad for us sometimes too, Good Laws, yes.'

He stopped. It was a memory he didn't want to discuss. After a pause he added, 'But if you've got faith, it'll pull you through!'

Lewis Jones, the tousle-haired former inhabitant of Sodom, looked on the battle between keepers and poachers more bitterly. He remembered one incident in Sodom Covert – the sprawling overgrown land that adjoins The Warren.

'One time, Evan Jones was netting rabbits when he bumped into some keepers. They tried to catch him, but others came to help. There was a big fight with no one knowing who they were hitting in the dark. Evan got hit bad on the head, but the others managed to get him away in the scuffle.

'The police were looking for them everywhere. Evan had to be hidden because of the big cut on his head. The others gave money to help him. But the keepers wanted to have somebody. In the end they took in one of their own men. He got jailed for two months – for bad character they called it. He hadn't even been there that night!'

I guessed that this episode must have been when the Nantlys estate carpentry shop suddenly closed down. It was run by Evan Jones for my family. The truth was that he couldn't appear at work with the wounds he had received in the woods the night before if he was to escape the keepers who were still looking for him. He had no choice but to go into hiding. My family – at least my grandfather – probably heard the truth, but Evan Jones, like Savage, was never caught. He remained in hiding in Sodom for years. He had lost his daytime respectability and never again spoke to my family. The estate carpentry shop never reopened.

Conservative Lizzie and Richard Hugh at Penuchaf apparently used older, quieter methods of catching rabbits that involved less risk and smaller profits. Richard Hugh snared time of Lizzie's death, twelve went by the name of Elizabeth Jones.

When she found Lizzie Penuchaf, she told me her nearest relation was a cousin, a woman who was living in St Asaph. This cousin, and another relation, a man who had appeared at Penuchaf suddenly one afternoon told me the strangest, saddest story of all that I had encountered.

Lizzie and Richard Hugh were the end of a family. Their father, David, had come from Llansannan in the hills a dozen miles away to the west. Their mother Ellen had belonged to a family that had lived in Tremeirchion as far back as the church records go. Ellen's mother Jane and father Edward had lived at Summerhill, a good farm with rich valley land, the same place that Savage Williams had set up residence in the barn. It seems likely that it was this couple who had run to Savage in the haystack to beg him for help.

Jane was remembered long after her death as beautiful and mysterious. Like her daughter Ellen, she had thick, dark hair. I was told that, until the birth of her children, she was the last of her family line. She had strong beliefs, but talked little about them. I wondered if she had been able to share anything with Ellen because Jane died suddenly when Ellen was only four, just after the birth of her third child, Elizabeth. Jane's husband, Edward, did not go into mourning because he was already deeply involved with Anne, who was carrying his child.

Only a few months after the death of Jane, Edward married Anne before the birth of his fourth child, also called Edward. Anne wasn't content with taking Jane's place; she had barely moved into Summerhill before she insisted that her three step-children, including Ellen, now five, John three, and baby Elizabeth be sent away. It isn't clear if their father put up any resistance. All that he can be given credit for is that the children weren't abandoned to the workhouse, but even there they would at least have been together.

A stranger arrangement was made. Each child was sent to a different house, not as an adopted child, but as an unpaid servant. Ellen was sent to Edward's brother, Hugh, who lived at Penuchaf on the mountain. In spite of Hugh being her uncle, Ellen was not taken in as his family, only as a domestic servant, as Hugh noted coldly in the 1871 census. John was sent thirteen miles away to a family who owned a grocery store in Rhyl, where he became 'a boots', a help in the shop and houseboy, and little Elizabeth was sent to a family in Holywell, thirteen miles away in another direction. It is hard to imagine any way in which these three children could have been made sadder and more isolated.

The tiny Elizabeth suffered the most. She was sent to Holywell before she was old enough to understand the humiliating deal which had been made, and never would understand why the family she lived with treated her as a servant for no pay. As soon as she was old enough, she fled to a convent and was renamed Sister Fidelio. Her miserable childhood haunted her; she was never healthy and died while still in her twenties at a sister branch of the North Wales convent in Birmingham.

Why were the children so ill-treated? Was it guilt – or even fear of the dead Jane? Is it possible Anne couldn't bear seeing her in the eyes of her children? Did she know that Jane was believed 'to have powers', not in the way of Miriam Crewe because of special insights she had, but by inheritance. Some of Jane's ancestors had eaten the flesh of wild eagles in a special ritual long ago that was believed still to give power over certain illnesses. If Anne thought she was safe without Jane's children at last, she was wrong.

Within five years of his second marriage, Edward Price was ruined and as destitute as Ellen, John and little Elizabeth. He had stood bond for another man, who was up on serious charges. The man vanished; Edward Price was called on to satisfy the bail. The amount of money was substantial. He was ruined. Paying that debt bankrupted him. He lost Summerhill and all his possessions less than ten years after Jane had died. Edward and Anne had to move to the backstreets of Holywell, where Edward ended his days as a lamplighter, one of the lowest paid jobs, usually given to boys who could run fast, lighting the old gas street lamps at dusk and extinguishing them at dawn. Even Anne's own grandchildren told the story as though justice was done.

It wasn't long before John and Ellen were each doing better than their father. John worked his way up in the store, until one day he came to own the business. It was his shop that sent out deliveries to Tremeirchion, and who Tom 'y go" had fooled one day. Ellen worked patiently at Penuchaf until she met David Jones, a man from Llansannan, at church one Sunday.

David was entirely Welsh. He never spoke English and could barely write it. He was not a flamboyant Welshman like Tom Williams from Pen-y-Maes, but a cool, quiet, reserved man, the sort of man who seemed to have a lot of strength inside, but it stayed inside. Whatever his talents were, they weren't for farming. He did that because that was the only work there was going around Llansannan. He worked for a big estate whose main house, Llewesog Hall, lay near Ruthin.

He was an intensely religious man. David and Ellen met at church. The religious and not so religious met at church, but David Jones and Ellen Price were serious churchgoers for all of their lives. Later, they attended all three services at Tremeirchion church each Sunday. They would have been there for Lester Jones' funeral. Lizzie followed their example, though there were fewer services. She sat up at the front, where the choir once would have sat, close to the altar.

After their marriage, Ellen moved from the village of her childhood servitude only to encounter more trouble in Llansannan. David got into a conflict with his employer, the local landlord, over Ellen, who the landlord said was supposed to work in the big house for his rent-free cottage, Rhyd Eidion.

Not only must David work, tending the horses, and harnessing them up to go and fetch provisions and agricultural supplies from Denbigh, but also his wife. Ellen had started to work in the main house, but soon wanted to stop, either because she didn't like it or because she found the work too hard with carrying her first baby. Their cottage wasn't even close to Llewesog Hall.

According to his landlord, there was a problem too about David and his care of the animals and his being anywhere on time. It seems he was not an early riser. When I first heard about the contents of the angry notes from his employer – they were all in Welsh – I didn't think much of David's inability to be anywhere on time. After my long conversation with Trevor Bryn Ffynnon, I knew what that meant. He'd probably been up too long the night before. John Rhewys told me David was good at poaching.

The acrimonious notes from Llewesog Hall got worse. David wrote back that the little tied cottage Rhyd Eidion was a wreck; David and Ellen had to leave. They returned to Penuchaf where old Hugh Price was alone after the death of his wife Elizabeth. He needed company, and apparently missed Ellen and her cheerful, gentle ways so much he was ready to take her back along with David and the baby Elizabeth, named after her aunt, Sister Fidelio. Hugh Price, who once called himself her employer, now made Ellen heir to all the furniture and pewter, china and clocks which had been in this house, and before that at the nearby house of Cae Gwyn, for more than three centuries.

Then Richard Hugh was born, and soon little Lizzie was ready to go to school. She started walking over the hilltop fields and down the old road between banks so high that the daylight never touched the ground but, like her grandmother Jane, Lizzie soon discovered that she was different. She took her books seriously, she loved the music that Harry England taught, she dreamt of becoming a pianist. Lizzie came to life in the classroom; in the playground she retreated. She appears in the school photo for the next dozen years or so. While the rest of the class seem to be looking out at the cameraman asking why he's there, what they can do to help him, or he them, Lizzie seems to be quietly hanging on to her own secrets.

Two years later, Richard Hugh joined her daily trips to and fro from the school. Brother and sister were model pupils. They worked hard, but they didn't play like the rest of the kids. In later life, Lizzie carefully preserved the leaflets of games for all the village celebrations. She loved the excuse to let her hair down when she trusted everyone around, but Richard Hugh wasn't like that. He was a shy, gentle boy. He didn't want to play, so the two of them never stayed behind after school, but quietly walked home up the hill to Penuchaf.

Richard Hugh loved learning. School was a treat for him. Within a few years Richard Hugh started collecting the annual prize for perfect attendance, as well as prizes for reading and mathematics. He loved figures and counting – their neatness, precision and orderliness.

At an early age Richard Hugh, as he would always be known, started helping his father on the farm, keeping records, writing down when the carthorse mare 'had taken a horse' as he put it, and when the foal was due, what crops they had sold and how much for, and even taking a few fat lambs down the hill to the pub on the way to school. In the days before refrigeration, the Salusbury Arms ordered lambs on the hoof as they needed them from Penuchaf. They were slaughtered, butchered and cooked on the premises.

At Penuchaf, Ellen worked hard on the farm and in the fields, but she was by no means masculine. She was a good-looking woman with thick, black hair, swept back full and tied in a small knot behind her head. She enjoyed dressing well and, from the photos and the contents of the drawers, it is clear she loved to buy hats and jet jewellery beads in long shiny strands from a big store in Liverpool. Ellen had a warm and generous personality, and Lizzie adored her. She also knew she had inherited an ability as a healer, and at least one relation came to stay in the belief that Ellen could help her recover from shingles.

Then, in the summer of 1914, war broke out. Richard Hugh was too young to fight, but he was drafted as soon as he was old enough, in January 1917. He was sent out to France, but the army sergeant soon realized that he would not be any use with a gun or a bayonet, and he was assigned to look after the horses, to be a driver and lead the horses moving the heavy artillery.

At regular intervals, Ellen sent parcels of food for which Richard Hugh thanked in his letters. One time, he acknowledged receiving some soap too, but it sounded as though he didn't know when he would next have a chance to use it. He must have been in the front lines, with little in the way of furloughs away from the fighting. As military regulations demanded, he wrote nothing of the war, but he looked at the French farmers and wondered how his father was coping without him. He reminded his father and questioned him whether he was keeping up with the planting.

Then, the team of horses with a gun carriage that he was leading took a direct hit. The horses were blown up, and Richard Hugh, who must have ducked just in time, barely survived. It was his specially assigned team of horses. According to John Rhewys, Richard Hugh never got over this. A week later, a card was sent to Penuchaf on which Richard Hugh had made a simple tick to reassure his family that he was still alive. Away from the front, his body recovered, and he was sent back up to the lines. When the war ended, Richard Hugh had the misfortune now to be still looking after the horses. While the other men were sent home, he was kept on because someone was needed to tend the animals until they had been dispersed. Finally, on 13 October 1919, he caught the train home. Some men in the village watched him return with interest. They said,

Meyriel Edge

The cast-iron front gate of Nantlys was designed to be an absolute barrier to rabbits, while providing an uninterrupted view of the park and hill on beyond.

I was even more puzzled. The 'drive gate' was the fine white gate at the front entrance of Nantlys. It was made out of closely spaced vertical iron bars, each topped with a spike that managed to be both ornamental and sharp. This strong gate was set in a brick wall three feet high that ran along the side of the garden facing the driveway and park. To the north, screening out the stableyard and track leading through to the fields below, the wall rose to ten feet high, while to the west lay the sunken fence or ha-ha. By the 1930s my family had almost certainly forgotten that the large garden had been built at great expense to exclude intruders – most notably the common rabbit – but clearly the gardeners and the rabbits who lived nearby had not.

Apparently, Mr Dyke's last task before going home on certain winter nights was to open the front gate. As soon as it was completely dark, Mr Dyke and Thomas Jones slipped back through the woods, following those long strands of dark woodland. They came right back into the garden that they tended by day, which would be now full of rabbits, and silently set their net loosely across the open gateway. It was crucial that the rabbits didn't know they were there – yet.

They had to wait for the right moment. And that depended on what my family were doing – the front gate was only twenty-five feet from the house. They could not do anything at a time when someone could hear what was happening outside and come to a window. So, ironically, they waited until the whole family were collected together in the room that is closest to the gate – the dining room – because that is when my family became most distracted, engrossed in each other's company and that evening's debate.

'We had to wait, crouching down right under the dining room window – that was the best part of all.' Mr Dyke's eyes gleamed with delight.

'We could hear everything and we got to know everyone – we could almost tell them by their footsteps. We had to count them in – you couldn't have one person left upstairs. We'd hear the bell for dinner and then Mr Pennant would come, then Mr David, then Miss Pennant, then Mrs Pennant – are they all there? No! There's another coming in – you'd hear the chairs go back. One, two, three, four – there's Mr Arthur coming now, five. Still one more – there he is now, Mr Philip – six. They're all there!

'We waited until they'd all started eating – then someone would say something that got them all talking.'

I knew exactly what he meant – those closely argued, thought-provoking discussions I had listened to as a child.

'Then one of us would tighten the wires at the gate and the other would go around behind. As soon as they saw us, the rabbits'd run straight back the way they'd come – through the gate of course and into the net. Then we had to get them up on our back and, quick as a light, up the park because of all the squealing.'

As Mr Dyke was talking I realized that on a dark night with

enough wind everyone was out there. It wasn't just the mean characters with a taste for violence and a grudge against their landlords. It was the recluses and the men who loved company alike, the kind and the cruel, the friendly and the hostile, the unemployed and the employed.

On a good night there was probably not a single able-bodied man in bed in Sodom. They were all out there, creeping through the pitch-black night, pushing quietly through the undergrowth, moving stealthily through the open woods, putting out their snares and checking them, carrying their huge long nets and then, at the end of the night, bumping into each other as they carried their nets and haul back up the mountain or to a secret drop-off point for the morning. Some were just learning, falling into each other's nets; others had been at it for half a century or more and knew as much as a human being will ever know about local wind patterns and the behaviour of rabbits and gamebirds in the area.

There wasn't a single man I interviewed who had lived in Sodom who didn't eventually describe the widespread network of night-time hunting – as soon as I started to laugh at the mention of 'rabbits'. That was all it took – all except for Dan Owen, the blind man who could no longer watch my face. But his father had apparently been the greatest poacher and storyteller of them all and the partner of the estate carpenter who, together, had brought long nets to Sodom.

During the day a man might be given a shilling as a beater to stir up game for a landlord's shooting party, but by night that same man would go out to collect some of the birds and animals that the landlords had missed with all their manpower and guns by day. There were two worlds in Sodom, the casual and haphazard activities of the day, and the real business of the night.

14

An absent-minded man

WHAT HAPPENED TO the families on the mountain who did not go out at night? Hugh Jones of Pen-y-Mynydd must have been one of those. If he did catch a few rabbits around his field, he did it as inefficiently as he did almost everything else in his life, and it made no difference. Hugh Jones, Pen-y-Mynydd, as he is always referred to, was the man people pointed to when they talked about the destitution of the hilltops.

Everyone loved Hugh. While many of his cannier neighbours were shrouded in mystery, Hugh was an open book. He was kind, intelligent, cheerful and improvident. In the many stories that circulate about Hugh, he seems to have been even poorer than his wife, known as 'Big Katharine' by their neighbours. She was several inches taller than her husband and more determined. Hugh was of below average height, thin, thoughtful and absent-minded.

The misfortunes of Hugh's family became legendary. Most people were sure he had at least a dozen children, but Miss Davies of Elwyd Uchaf was emphatic – 'only five girls and one boy', she declared. After many years of marriage, as Hugh shrank under the burden of obligations he never managed to fulfil, Kate seemed to grow, becoming larger, more determined and more threatening. And yet, even with all her determination to get away from the poverty that gripped them, Katharine failed to change their way of life.

Hugh Jones knew the Bible intimately, reading large portions of it each day. Christianity ran deep in his veins. He helped to administer the chapel which he and his family attended every Sunday, come rain or shine, but it was an unpaid position.

Instead of going out at night with traps or nets, he and his family often sang hymns.

'They'd all sit down and have potatoes for supper, just boiled potatoes – they didn't have anything else – and when that was finished, they'd sing. They'd be there singing hymns till well past midnight. You could hear them as you went by. They had wonderful voices.

'Well, next morning, of course, they wouldn't be up on time. You'd see Katharine going by in such a hurry, rushing along the road, and you'd know she was going to miss the train – the only one – to market. And she did!' Trevor chuckled.

Hugh Jones, Pen-y-Mynydd, became famous for not having his mind on what he was doing. 'He used to do some very funny things,' Dan Owen recounted.

'One time, when his cow was dry, and he had to get some milk for his children from Dan's family, Hugh was coming up the worst of the gradient just above Bryn Goleu when the old pony stopped. He had a load of straw on his cart and the pony pulling up front – and he was holding on to the can of milk. When the old pony stopped, Hugh jumped out and, instead of finding a stone, he slipped the can behind the wheel to stop the cart running back down the hill and losing straw, cart, pony and all.

'In a great white splash, the milk poured out down the hill. Hugh turned around and walked alone a quarter of a mile back down the slope to ask for some more milk. When he got to Gwern Hwlcyn, he realized the can was still stuck under the cartwheel and so he had to ask for a jug too.'

This story, like others about Hugh, rapidly travelled the neighbourhood. Another time, everyone was sick with flu and Hugh and Katharine were beside themselves with worry for their children. To save taking all six sick children to the doctor, something they couldn't afford, the doctor suggested Hugh bring in urine specimens for each child. Hugh and Katharine collected all the specimens in an assortment of bottles and jars topped off with brown paper and string but, by the time Hugh had travelled the five miles to Denbigh in his pony and trap, he couldn't remember which jar or bottle belonged to which child. So he had to go back and start all over again.

The only thing that anyone can remember Hugh Jones doing for a living is growing carrots. 'They grew well in the sandy soil.' The only problem was that rabbits did too – they loved to build their burrows in the soft sandy soil. The rabbits used to be abundant in the great expanse of scrub that thrived on the steep slopes of Sodom. The scrub ran right alongside Hugh's field of carrots.

All that remained in 1984 of the inglenook or *aelwyd* around which Hugh Jones sang hymns with his family. The tiny house appears to have been only one small room with a byre across an internal passage for their cow and chickens.

154

As everyone who has tried to grow carrots around rabbits knows, rabbits love carrots, and just one rabbit can eat off the tops of a lot of carrots in one night. Maybe Hugh was cleverer than his neighbours realized, and he was growing the carrots to trap the rabbits quite legitimately in the field he farmed. But even this didn't go right. Perhaps he was too late, or his neighbours got there first, because Hugh never managed to get by in the same way as his neighbours did.

Hugh's life was such a shambles that he frequently came down to Nantlys to ask my grandfather for help or advice. My uncles remembered seeing him driving down in his old shandry pulled by a cob. The simple platform on which he stood made it look as if he was driving an ancient chariot of war.

Most of the people who came and went to Nantlys in those days walked up and down the hill because these slopes were perilous with a horse and cart, as Hugh knew well. But Hugh always drove, standing on the float behind his pony, presumably because he was always late or short of time.

Hugh had everyone's sympathy and he, in turn, loved his neighbours. Seeing Hugh standing behind his pony driving down to Nantlys made everyone sad too – they knew that some new disaster had befallen the family at Pen-y-Mynydd.

*

When I was clearing out Lizzie's house, among all the cards, letters of condolence, scrawled notes and letters written by her brother Richard Hugh from the trenches of the First World War, there were several others that stood out. The writing was fine, almost the writing of a gentleman who had been taught careful calligraphy by a private tutor. These letters were full of observations and unusual pondering, which had got past the strict army censors – they were from Hugh Jones, Pen-y-Mynydd.

Apparently, Hugh was one of the few people who became

close friends with the family from Penuchaf, though they were not related. The two families had a lot in common. Like Richard Hugh, Hugh Jones got no thrills from feats of daring with the nets at night. They didn't need the hill for camouflage.

From his letters Hugh Jones appears to have been the best educated man in Sodom, 'and he had clever children too', John Rhewys Morris told me. Though Sodom seemed to be so primitive, many of its inhabitants were not lacking in intelligence. Lewis Jones, a gruff man with long sandy-grey hair that went this way and that the day I called in on him remembered his grandfather 'always had a book in his hand'.

In houses where people slept as many as ten to a room, there was plenty of education and intellect. It wasn't true that the people of Sodom were unable to compete in the valley for work. It was more that they had a different way of seeing things and preferred the freedom of Sodom.

Their seclusion vanished with the draft during the First World War. For the first time in their lives, against all the quiet traditions of their families, these men found themselves in camps of hundreds and thousands being trained and then sent on to the crowded filthy trenches of the front lines.

While he was in France, Hugh Jones wrote back regularly to the family at Penuchaf, telling them about his thoughts and about the war. He was frustrated that he was stationed only a mile or two from Richard Hugh, yet they were never allowed to meet. Hugh kept forecasting the end of the war. He was forever noticing hopeful signs and managed to communicate a good deal without having his letters marked by the censors.

In August 1918, after three years of being almost continuously in the shelling of the front lines, he was still able to write, 'It has been very nice weather here this last month, but it's changing a little today. We have had a nice shower of rain.

'The French are very good farmers in their ways – quite a different way to Wales. They haven't hardly no men to work, so it's women who do the greater part of the work. They seem quite used to working in the fields.

'There is very good news these days. It will be at an end before our Hugh is ready. I believe that Stephen [a cousin/ nephew] has been very lucky. He is at base now.'

Presumably, Stephen was in the field hospital having just missed being killed by a shell. Hugh continued, 'They have a different churn here to ours and different machinery...'

Was Hugh Jones steering nimbly past the censor's black ink, which never touched his letters, or was he wanting to save the family at Penuchaf from the pain of the Front, or was this simply his way?

Trevor Jones, Bryn Ffynnon, remembered, one snowy winter, seeing Hugh's cob coming through the snow over the top of Sodom.

'It was a big snow. The pony could hardly go and there was Katharine leading the pony along, with Hugh standing in the cart holding the baby that was sick.'

It was soon after this that Katharine made up her mind. She decided they had had enough of life on the mountain and living in Wales. They would emigrate to Canada.

But Hugh didn't want to go. He didn't want to leave. Hugh loved Wales – Canada held nothing for him that he needed. He loved Pen-y-Mynydd where he had grown up, but as new troubles and sickness came their way, he finally had to let Katharine have her way.

According to my uncle, my grandfather wrote a letter or gave the whole family the money to get to Canada. Everyone in the surrounding area knew of their departure. Many families left quietly, bitter at the troubles they had endured – but not Katharine and Hugh.

First, there was a sale of what little they had at Pen-y-Mynydd. Then, 'they left from Caerwys station. There was a huge crowd too to see them off, even Herbert Lewis [the local MP] came!'

It was an occasion that people didn't forget. Hugh Jones and his family came early to the station and his whole family stood on the platform and sang one last time to the whole crowd of friends and neighbours. Hugh broke down and wept.

'He didn't want to go.'

Hugh and his family crossed the Atlantic in steerage, deep in the bowels of a luxury ocean liner. Almost all the way they sang Welsh airs to entertain their fellow passengers.

When Hugh got to the other side of the Atlantic, some people said the family went to Manitoba, someone else said to Newfoundland, but my uncle, who seemed to have quite precise information on this, said that Hugh and his family were taken into the interior to Saskatchewan at the expense of the Canadian Pacific Railroad and settled on railway property out there. As soon as they arrived at their destination on the Great Plains, the family put down their bags and sang once more.

Hugh's children did well in Canada, and several went on to join a profession. His son was able to travel back to Wales with his family to tell the story of the crossing, but, for Hugh, Canada was not at all like Wales. He died within a short time of his arrival at the age of only fifty.

In Sodom they said he had died of a broken heart.

15

How it all ended

THOUGH GOING OUT with the nets by night was risky enough, selling the night's catch by day was harder. The Poaching Prevention Act of 1862 ordered stiff penalties for anyone caught as much as transporting rabbits if he wasn't the owner of a large amount of land. On the public highways police were empowered to search whomever they suspected.

The task of taking the rabbits to sell was almost always shouldered by the women. In some families husbands took rabbits and game to the village shop under cover of darkness, while their wives walked down on market day and picked up these bags and caught the bus that ran from outside the shop. That way, no one was seen walking down from Sodom with any bulky packages in daylight.

Lizzie Jones of Penuchaf preferred to have no accomplices. So she walked all the way to Denbigh with her mysterious two-tiered basket 'with four or five rabbits in the bottom and butter and a few eggs laid out neatly over the top'. The butter and eggs all wrapped in a clean white cloth would have looked a picture of innocent and modest husbandry, but the basket must have weighed nearly twenty pounds, no small burden to carry six miles each week. It took its toll on her back. By the end of her life her spine was badly curved and she moved forward walking in the shape of a strange S-hook.

In Denbigh dealers bid for the rabbits. They came mostly from Birkenhead, which faces across the Mersey to Liverpool, the nearest large city to North Wales. From Birkenhead rabbits and other black market game were distributed throughout the north of England. A gamekeeper pointed out, 'Poor people in all the big towns, their main meat was rabbit cooked all sorts of different ways... Even the big hotels bought rabbit and served it as chicken.'

In Denbigh the trading of rabbits and other game all took place not in the main market place but in a back street, which was notorious for poachers. Many of them lived there, surviving entirely on their forays into neighbouring estates. A keeper told me, 'If you went down by day, you'd see all the nets out to dry and the men'd be there picking twigs out of them.' Another keeper's son said keepers hardly dared to walk down that street alone a few decades ago.

Denbigh market day was the social event of the week for the farming community that stretches out in every direction from this old fortified town. The town covers a small conical hill that tilts back towards the moorland, and was originally fortified by Wales' cherished ruler, Llywelyn the Great. When Edward I conquered Wales two generations later, he built a new castle that still stands at the top of the hill.

In Lizzie's time, everyone came on the same day, the farmers with their animals, the women with dairy products, eggs and vegetables, and more than a few with heavy, well-packed bundles. The long market square was full to bursting with stalls, animals and people chatting.

Farmers scrutinized each other's cattle, lambs and pigs, all penned up waiting for the auctioneer. They also offered advice, discussed the weather and told stories. But the most important topic at market day was always prices, the price lambs were making that week compared to last, whether they were improving; if not, why not, and what price lamb was fetching at other Welsh and English markets that week. It was a bottomless topic. On the basis of swings in prices, each farmer had to decide when to sell his own stock to make the best price. If he sold early, his livestock would not weigh so much; if he waited too long he might end up selling in a glut.

To cater to this strong local public interest, *The Denbighshire Free Press* published the average prices in each category every week. In January 1909 they listed the current price for every type of animal, wool, butter and eggs, but never mentioned rabbits. By 1919 the trade was so well known that rabbits were added to the bottom of the list. In that year rabbits were selling for three to four shillings per couple. In other words, if you could sell ten or a dozen rabbits in a week, you could earn more than a full-time agricultural worker.

The rabbit trade was flourishing, but it was only good as long as the cold weather lasted and the rabbits would keep fresh during their journey to Birkenhead. Mr Dyke pointed out, 'You could only sell them from September to March. They wouldn't buy them in the summer. You couldn't give them away then!'

Later, particularly with the introduction of long nets and the quantities becoming too much for women to carry, buyers from Birkenhead drove around country lanes in unmarked vans to special pick-up points. One of these pick-up points was on the grass verge directly opposite the entrance to Nantlys. An unmarked black van stopped there well into the 1950s.

On one occasion we were all in the car, and my father was told to get out to find out who the van belonged to and what it was doing there. He was reluctant and came back soon. 'There wasn't anybody there,' he reported. Apparently, they were all hiding behind the wall, alerted by a look-out that my family's car was coming up our long bumpy drive.

This was the most convenient place to collect the rabbits from Tom Jones, the ferreter, and the family whose children checked the snares on the way to school. The children of this family were delegated to do the selling as well. One of them remembers bitterly, 'Everyone was afraid – they were in such a difficult position with the rabbits. People were so afraid. They were so vulnerable.'

The rabbits that were not sold were bartered for food and work, and consumed in quantity up in Sodom. Mr Dyke remembers, 'We lived on rabbits. Just got tea and bread from the village. Otherwise it was rabbits every day. Boiled, roast, every way you can think of. I like rabbit pie the best. I don't know what they used to do. They'd never tell you. Just "Do you like it?" is all they'd say. My son was brought up on rabbit – plenty of meat. That's why he's so strong and bigger than all the rest.'

At over six feet Mr Dyke's son, Donald, was one of the tallest men in Tremeirchion. Since men started growing crops in prehistoric times, Sodom must have been one of the few places in the world where meat, not starch, was the most available food.

Sodom wasn't an agricultural community, but a hunting one. Rabbits provided both food and money. The economy of Sodom was rabbits, yet this, the main activity of the area, was clandestine and so skilfully carried out that only rumours reached the valley and even the keepers had no idea of the scale of operations on the mountain.

But the days of rabbiting on Sodom came to an abrupt end when I was a few years old. In the early 1950s a new disease spread from the south of England, reaching the Vale of Clwyd in 1954. It was myxomatosis – fatal to rabbits and so contagious and deadly that almost no rabbit seemed able to resist or recover from the disease. Sick rabbits returned to their burrows to die and the disease spread through every warren.

The disease appalled even the farmers who had cursed rabbits for eating their crops. Suddenly, the countryside was full of dying rabbits. Along all the country roads there were rabbits flopping up and down or kicking helplessly, squealing with pain. Death from myxomatosis was drawn out over several days, even weeks, and intensely painful. The nose, ears, eyelids and even genitalia became so grotesquely swollen that people said the rabbits were blowing up and bursting like balloons. Their tall, acutely sound-sensitive ears were so weighted down with fluid that they lolled pathetically around each rabbit's head.

A feeling of mourning, mixed with anger and frustration, spread throughout the countryside at this disease which was introduced deliberately by a few farmers from Australia. My parents tried to prevent us from seeing all the dying rabbits. We stopped going for walks, and they tried to distract us whenever we drove past the animals dying along the sides of the roads. It seemed that the rabbits had lost all their natural shyness and were deliberately exposing themselves to human beings and danger to try to escape their pain.

'When the myxi came,' Trevor Jones, Bryn Ffynnon, remembered, 'the rabbits even came into the yard. I'd never seen a rabbit close to the house before. The same rabbits we'd been chasing all these years came right up to us, but this time their eyes were bulging, they were staring right at us and not running away. I believe they were looking for someone to knock them over the head and put them out of their misery. Even the cats walked away from them.

'I finished off all the ones I found and buried the dead ones I found too, but there was nothing to be done, the myxi kept on going.'

The young man who had caught rabbits as a child said, 'We were living off rabbits, but then the myxomatosis came and there were no more rabbits. We stayed for another two or three years, but we couldn't live. That's what did it.'

Trevor Jones said finally, 'Why everyone left the mountain? There were plenty of people left before the myxi came. But afterwards they had nothing to eat. Everyone was living off rabbits, though no one said as much. There used to be a lot of people and then suddenly the mountain was all quiet.'

At last I knew what had happened in those murky intense years of my early childhood. I had been right, something strange had happened – an extraordinary community had suddenly disappeared because of a new rabbit disease. In telling his story, the one Trevor had wanted to tell for so long, he had given me that missing link in my life. After that, the longest interview we ever had, I felt we could both sit comfortably alone in silence. Though we had known different lives, we had no secrets, and I think he trusted me as much as I did him. I was no longer an outsider in Wales. I felt I belonged at last, as much as anyone ever belongs in that strange wild landscape.

16

Older tunes

If you follow the twisting, single-track lane around the back of Cefn Du from Sodom crossroads, leaving Bryn Goleu on the other side of the hill, past the ruins of Hugh Jones' old house, on curling around the darker side of the summit back towards Tremeirchion, you cross the old droving roads heading to Caerwys and Newmarket. Then you come to Penuchaf and Pant Glas, where Johnny Roberts and his wife did not bother with washing up; they just threw the dregs in the fire and turned the teacups over when the Jones' from Penuchaf visited.

Almost opposite Pant Glas was the little farm of Pen-y-Maes: a collection of fields on the flat lands behind the crest of the hills above Tremeirchion. The Williams' of Pen-y-Maes owned this farm. They were beholden to no one. They were the closest neighbours and best friends of the family at Penuchaf. Lizzie's mother Ellen went over to dig potatoes with Eleanor Williams, and the Williams' came back to help the Jones' in their harvest and enjoy the harvest supper, with gravy, grey and thick as mud.

But Eleanor Williams died young, probably in childbirth, and her husband was unable to support his family on this small farm without her. Wretched, he left Tremeirchion to go and work in the mines near Wrexham. His daughter Annie broke her arm climbing over a gate and never recovered. Mr Williams had to sell his land, field by field. Each field he sold, he named for one of his children, right down to the last one, Cae Annie. Mr Williams held on to the tiny house and gave it to his son Tom, who promised he would return. The family left. Tom emigrated to America and did well in San Francisco. He wrote back often to Lizzie and Richard Hugh about how much he missed Tremeirchion and life on the hilltops, but as the decades passed, his tone changed and he begged them to leave, too. He thought their lives were too hard.

Tom wasn't alone. Everyone in the village – almost everyone agreed. Lizzie and Richard Hugh had got to move. What was keeping them there in the old house with no telephone, no bath, no indoor sanitation, not even running water, only an old Victorian coal grate to cook on and not even a decent track up to the house? The old driveway was overgrown with trees and tree roots, tall grass and thistles. Only people in this village knew there was even a house across the fields.

All I knew was that Lizzie and her simple way of life was far more interesting and attractive than anything I saw elsewhere. The Jones' were living by their own lights. I only wished I could get to know them, but I was a child, and they were an elderly, reclusive couple – welcoming, but so reticent.

Then Richard Hugh died in 1972, followed by Lizzie four years later. My father, as executor, allowed me to turn out the house and sell the contents. Following the terms of Lizzie's will the proceeds were given to charity. It was only then that I started asking questions. Lizzie's closest neighbour, John Rhewys Morris of Mynydd Bychan, told me that the Jones' were special – they lived by a different code. No idea as to why.

And so I went to the nursing home where Lizzie had died and talked to the matron who told me that Lizzie was a loner, even there. She had a chair that she chose, and that was the only place she wanted to sit. When she looked up Lizzie in her book, we found that amongst the seventy residents there at the rabbits in the fields that he rented from Nantlys – which was his right. But he did it so furtively that it seems he never knew or had confidence in that right. He worked in great secrecy and wouldn't have anybody with him.

In another family the children were put to work. One man remembered putting down snares on his way to school, then checking them and collecting the rabbits on the way home. Yet another way of catching rabbits, without resorting to the tell-tale sound of guns, was to send trained ferrets into the burrows to drive the rabbits out into waiting nets.

One of the gardeners at Nantlys, who had grown up in Sodom, was an expert with ferrets. Even when he moved down to the valley to live at the lodge by the top drive gate of Nantlys, Thomas Jones took his ferrets with him. As children we were fascinated by these extraordinary wiry animals, with bodies scarcely broader than an old English penny. In spite of their size, ferrets are immensely strong. A single animal could kill and drag a rabbit many times its own weight.

'Rabbiting' with ferrets only worked, however, if you could block or net all the different exits to the burrow the ferret was put into, and if your ferret was well trained to chase and not to kill.

Training ferrets and netting the burrows involved so much skill and patience that few poachers bothered with it.

But Tom trained his ferrets well, and could work out the intricacies of a rabbit warren. Tom Jones claimed his ferrets were for catching moles, but he never showed them off when my parents were around. I sometimes heard my parents discussing the enormous amount of molehills in the park near the lodge, and how Thomas Jones seemed completely incompetent with his ferrets.

Not only was Tom Jones better with ferrets than anyone else in the neighbourhood, he was also a crack shot with a catapult. At harvest time rabbits and other game frequently got stranded in the centre of a field of corn as the cutter circled the field working in from the edge. Apparently, Tom could hit five rabbits out of five as they broke cover almost simultaneously from the last few yards of standing corn.

Hearing this made me chuckle. To my family Thomas Jones was a kind, gentle man who seemed to take forever to finish even the simplest task. But that apparently was just his daytime persona.

In the 1930s Thomas Jones worked with Mr Dyke in the garden and on the farm at Nantlys. Mr Dyke was another man with a reputation like Thomas Jones in my family. He was obviously not slow-witted, and yet he was unpredictable – even more than Thomas Jones. No one felt sure quite what he was thinking. By the time I was a child he only worked for my parents on rare occasions. But his son still worked for my family when I moved into the cottage on the hill and he told me to go up and see his father, just as Eifion had, if I wanted to know about the old days.

John Dyke was happy to talk. He had recently moved to a house in Tremeirchion but had lived in Sodom before that. He talked about Miriam Crewe and Mrs Jones, Bryn Goleu, and, when he discovered that I knew the secret, he cheerfully told me more and explained the economics of poaching.

Mr Dyke explained, 'We got thirty-one shillings a week [in wages] and then there was seven pence for the stamp [National Insurance contribution] and five shillings for the rent. That didn't leave much for a family to live on. So we caught rabbits in the winter to make up the money. We even used to net them down by the Hall.'

He grinned broadly and then tried to change the subject but I asked, making use of my new-found knowledge, 'Where were "the runs" down there?' Mr Dyke dissolved into side-splitting laughter. He rocked to and fro until I thought his spindle-legged chair would break apart. Tears welled into his eyes. Even though we were the only people in his house, he leant forward and whispered, 'We used to drive them into nets in the drive gate.'

'The army will make a man of him. He'll be different now. He'll have to be.'

But Richard Hugh had not become more sociable; if anything, he became more reclusive. His cousin came to stay, and took him down to hang out by the bench on the hill at the end of the day to chat. People thought this was a change for the better, but after his cousin left, Richard Hugh did not return.

David Jones watched his two children and wondered why neither seemed intent on meeting people of the opposite sex. Lizzie enjoyed the Girls' Friendly Society, but Richard Hugh was always a loner. He enjoyed his work and reading. He used to stay outside late, reading with a lamp.

There was already plenty to do at Penuchaf for both Lizzie and Richard Hugh because neither David nor Ellen was well. Ellen suffered from severe stomach pains. Even lay people in those days knew what that could be. They watched as she grew worse. As the years passed, the visits to the doctor grew more frequent, and finally Richard Hugh noted £5 for a bottle of brandy, which was usually all people on the hill got for pain then. Ellen died in January 1927, and David survived for only three more winters before he died of pneumonia with meningitis. Lizzie and Richard Hugh were like two children who had never left home. People wondered how they would cope now. Strangely, they coped better than ever before.

Richard Hugh got a new vigour that he hadn't had since before he went to the war and started keeping immaculate account books, detailing every expense and income from the years after Ellen died. His accounts, now in the Flintshire Record Office, show exactly how much an old-fashioned but hard-working small hill farm could make from sixty acres in the 1930s, but one source of income that doesn't appear in any of their records was the earnings from rabbits. Apparently, Richard Hugh always worked alone, using nets and snares.

In 1930, Lizzie followed her brother's example and started keeping a full account of all her butter and egg sales. She was taking so many eggs to market that it is hard to see how she could have carried them all six miles to Denbigh, almost all of which would have been on foot. Were some of these eggs in fact rabbits? Lizzie was using her special basket with a deep lower compartment and two lids which closed down to make a shallow, upper compartment. In the top, Lizzie put all her butter and eggs wrapped in clean linen, and in the bottom four or even five rabbits. It would have been the 'egg' money that Lizzie used on her way home to buy the groceries at the Tan-y-Graig shop, before climbing the grassy drovers' road back to Penuchaf. However it was calculated, both up and down the mountain, she carried a full load.

Richard Hugh carefully worked the figures through. He started with £20 in his account in 1921. By 1932 he had saved £853, and, by the time he died his savings amounted to £5,500. Brother and sister never withdrew any money once deposited. Lizzie sold just enough rabbits in winter to pay for all their immediate needs, and Richard Hugh sold enough livestock in summer to cover all their farming expenses, but Richard Hugh's books showed that they shouldn't have been able to save so much. There should have been some withdrawals for living expenses.

When the Second World War broke out, the great energy Richard Hugh had had right through the 1930s disappeared. It seems that the horror of life in the trenches of the First World War crept back into his bones and made him unable to function. He kept no accounts whatsoever. He preserved few of his bills. It seems he even stopped catching rabbits – the deposits in his bank book declined. He went on with the old routines, but there was a big difference in efficiency.

Because of food shortages during the First World War, the starvation that had made Margaret Edwards shout across the valley at Lord Devonport's empty shooting lodge, a committee was set up in 1939, supposedly to aid farmers to be more productive, to make sure that the same thing couldn't happen again. Amongst several proposals adopted by the committee to safeguard the national food supply was a plan to inspect every farm across the country for efficiency. The plan got underway slowly.

The inspectors didn't get to Penuchaf until 1943 or '44. They made notes of exactly which crops were being or had been grown in each field. Richard Hugh didn't like the inquiry and was uncooperative from the start. Penuchaf was marked down as 'D', an 'A' being a farm efficiently run; a 'D' being a fail. Many farms didn't get an 'A' in Tremeirchion, including my family's own farm, Nant Gwilym. The inspector, who was supposed to be a sympathetic farmer, clearly had a better understanding of the valley farms, and he had quotas to fill. On the fertile flat land you could choose whether to put hay or crops or livestock in most fields.

A fight broke out between the inspector and Richard Hugh, particularly with regard to one field called Cae Bonkin. The inspector ordered Richard Hugh to plant a crop in Cae Bonkin, but, as his neighbour John Rhewys pointed out, 'it didn't make sense'. Richard Hugh ignored the inspector and left his sheep running over Cae Bonkin. The inspector returned to check each farm that had not got an 'A' grade first time around. Nant Gwilym passed a few shades under average, but when the inspector drove up the lonely mountain road to Penuchaf in August 1944, he found a herd of sheep grazing peacefully in Cae Bonkin, and not only that but, though the hay was cut and stowed in the barn, 'the corn was still standing... but not all of it... some of it... so a good proportion of it, in fact, was no longer there'. It had been eaten by the rabbits. Gradually working in from the edge of each field, they had chewed their way through row after row.

The inspector visiting the field didn't walk into the middle. He came through the gate and looked at the outer edges. What he saw made it look like someone had done several rounds with the harvester, leaving just some struggling stalks for yards and yards around the edge of the field. Richard Hugh's neighbours said the corn in the middle was still good, but what the inspector glared at was the edge.

It seems Richard Hugh was only taking rabbits for his own needs and, though rabbit catchers invaded each other's territories, everyone respected the limits of Penuchaf. The inspector was angry, and, instead of being mild as Richard Hugh was at every other occasion of his life, he exploded. He went ballistic, the anger of a lifetime and even more poured out. The inspector took to his heels; Penuchaf flunked again.

The War Agricultural Committee told Richard Hugh that he was not fit to farm sixty acres of Great Britain at a time of war. He had to leave. My father, as landlord, received the same notice, namely that Penuchaf was to be rented to another farmer who was more cooperative. Richard Hugh and Lizzie were thunderstruck. It had never occurred to Richard Hugh that in getting rid of the nosy inspector, they could lose Penuchaf. All he wanted was to be left in peace, and now they had ordered him to leave.

My father saw what was happening. He contacted the War Ag Committee, as it was called, but the answer was no. No changes could be made. The order had been given. My father visited Lizzie and Richard Hugh, and a new relationship began between the Jones' and my family. My father, who had had to give up a research position at Cambridge due to an unexplained paralysis, was at his best in a situation where everyone else had given up. He talked to Richard Hugh. He talked to Lizzie. He asked for time, which was granted.

Finally, my father came up with the solution. Lizzie and Richard Hugh would stay at Penuchaf and manage the farm, which would be joined to Nant Gwilym. The War Ag Committee agreed and probably never went near Penuchaf and its diminutive, but fiery, farmer again. Richard Hugh continued to keep sheep, but he dispersed all of his cows, carthorses and pigs over the next few years. Lizzie even gave up the hens.

By the time the solution was found, the Second World War was virtually at an end, but food rationing would continue for more than five years. The order was not rescindable. There was a valuation – a strange affair where negotiators for both sides met to discuss the current value of livestock and crops at Penuchaf. Richard Hugh had sold all of his cows by then – the valuation came in at only £393 for crops and what was left of his sheep.

The first visits I made to Penuchaf that I can remember would have been around 1956. I took one look at Lizzie's shining eyes and quiet but sure way of doing things and knew that she, above all the other people in the village, fascinated me – but I didn't know why. I knew only that I liked her for her open friendliness to our family, her lack of fear and her air of knowing a great deal more than she would ever say. Lizzie, I thought, had a story to tell.

Though the valley changed with new houses, new roads and new coinage, Penuchaf was just the same. If you went up there, you could be sure to find Lizzie and her smiling welcome. Richard Hugh looked after everything at Penuchaf, fed the cattle. If anything, Penuchaf produced less now, though some corn was grown and harvested with more modern machinery, and then whenever there was more going on down at Nant Gwilym, Richard Hugh walked over the hilltop and down the old drovers' track. He was always there for the harvests. One time, he was the last man in the field apart from a family guest, a bachelor called Gerry Crewdson. Gerry remembered when he and Richard Hugh finished the final stook in the deep summer dark; they quietly shook hands, man to man, congratulating each other.

Whenever I met him, Richard Hugh would beat a retreat. He would smile and start chattering in a funny, incomprehensible way which wasn't Welsh, before I ever got close enough to be able to ask a question. No one ever tried to get into a conversation with Richard Hugh in those days, but whenever we met, his face was wreathed in smiles. You couldn't miss him at a distance because he was much shorter than everyone else, and he always wore the same old black jacket, which shined like leather from the oil of all the sheep he had sheared and the grease of all the tractors he had repaired.

He carried his mountain reserve with him. He was there and not there at the same time. But we, as a family, visited the mountain more often – my mother, with my sister and I on our ponies. And so began my first relationship with anyone who lived on the mountain. I always wanted to learn more about the hilltops, but other people just nodded their heads, acknowledging they knew who I was, but there was no chance of a normal conversation. Lizzie and Richard Hugh were different. We became some of the very few people who visited Penuchaf, not that Lizzie ever volunteered a single detail about her life, but she in particular welcomed us into her mysterious kitchen.

It was the 1950s. Country oak furniture, which had been a specialist field since the 1890s, when it first started to be collected, was increasing in value. The old dressers that had stood in every Tremeirchion kitchen up to the 1930s were disappearing. Dealers and tinkers were taking every opportunity to buy up these pieces of furniture, up to two hundred years old, and most people were accepting their offer and replacing the dressers with modern cupboards. Dressers involved so much dusting, but the Penuchaf kitchen remained untouched. A local dealer knew about Penuchaf and approached Lizzie and Richard Hugh, but they were not interested in selling a thing.

For the most part, no one knew Penuchaf existed. With each decade, it became more of a secret. Lizzie and Richard Hugh's old friends had died or emigrated, fewer people went there, fewer people were welcome, but because of my father and the memory of my great-grandfather, whenever we went we were treated as old friends as we entered the dark kitchen with its rows of polished blue-and-white plates, its rack of pewter, the old Bible box and a miniature wooden desk, the Victorian ornaments that Hugh and Elizabeth Price had collected, and the small copy of the portrait of my great-grandfather. Lizzie was always enigmatic, asking questions, knowing what people might want to talk about, always keeping the conversation moving, especially when anyone wanted to ask her a question. She would barely answer the question of how she was.

Then, in 1972, Richard Hugh fell gravely ill – an ambulance was called – it would come the next day. Perhaps the driver didn't want to chance coming across the field at night. The vicar went up and asked if he could sit up with her until the ambulance came. Lizzie tried to brush him off, saying he wouldn't want to pass the night in a strange old place like that. Richard Hugh died a few weeks later.

Lizzie's inner power emerged then. Up until this point, she was devoted to her brother, but she hardly seemed to mourn. She carried on as before. It was as if Richard Hugh hadn't gone. His great coat from the First World War still hung behind the door. He all but remained alive. She didn't need her brother; she remembered him. But the pressure mounted for Lizzie to leave Penuchaf. Tom wrote again from San Francisco. The vicar said it was a scandal, having her still fetch water from the spring in the yard, but she wanted things as they were. She loved every stone of Penuchaf. The iron she had been given remained in its box. The television wasn't turned on any more. Her own health began to deteriorate.

The visiting nurse ordered that she be put in a nursing home, but Lizzie demanded to go home. She stayed at Penuchaf for one more summer. Then, in November, she was moved to the nursing home again. My father invited me to go and visit her with him. She was just as welcoming, but spoke little. I saw the delicate way my father questioned and reassured her. This time she stayed, but even now she carved out her own separate world. She died just as the new lambs were beginning to play games again in the fields around Penuchaf.

In my last interview with her, Sarah Parry, who had once 'read the tea', told me shyly about the belief regarding eagle's flesh, and it dawned on me, just as Jane had inherited the power, and Ellen too had, so would her only daughter have inherited that special power. It appears probable that Lizzie never practised her power visibly, but, at last, Sarah Parry told me that Lizzie knew she had the inherited special healing powers. She was indeed different – a last survivor of something very ancient.

Eagles have occupied no special place in any recent mythology, but to the Celts they were one of the most powerful and revered of the wild creatures of Europe. Many of the tribes of France carried eagles into battle as their sacred emblem. In defeating those tribes, the Roman legions took the emblem back to Rome as one of the many spoils of the Gallic Wars, and the eagle became the symbol of imperial Rome, a symbol of military prowess, the eagle as a symbol of healing power lost.

This bird was sacred to earlier shamans and druids, not to be eaten for food, but on occasion when some of the powers attributed to eagles were needed, an eagle would be caught, a near impossible feat without the use of a gun, and people ate its flesh and so were given beneficial powers including, it seems or came to be believed, powers over certain illnesses. Lizzie was one of, if not the last, conscious descendant of the people involved in these special rites – the last druid in a way.

Postscript

My father died in 1993 in a nursing home, on what he had long since decided was the site of Llywelyn's medieval *plas* in the Bodfari gap. Then in 2004, my mother was killed in a car accident. Nantlys was left to my sister and me. As a family we fell apart; we couldn't come close to a plan to keep it going. It was put on the market. The buyer wanted the house cleared, and so began the task of clearing out those forty rooms right down to the last broken toy.

In my father's study I found a game-book for 1906, and discovered that my family too shot rabbits by day and, sometimes, in small quantities, gave them to the farmer of the land where they were shot. A few would have been consumed at Nantlys. The rest? Apparently, even the keepers were selling rabbits. Trevor Jones, Bryn Ffynnon, had been right. Everyone was in on this game.

Towards the end of my research in the 1980s I learned that Lizzie and her mother Ellen were believed to have inherited special healing powers because their ancestors had eaten the flesh of wild eagles, but eagles have not flown over this part of Wales for centuries. I wondered how long Ellen's family had guarded the memory of this pagan feast.

Then I remembered how Lizzie had been a healing presence in my young life, which led to my fascination with her and her house and this story. When I was doing my research, I wanted to know if the ancient religions of Wales had survived on the mountain. In small ways they had, but by then I found that I didn't have to go up the mountain to tumble into the deeper worlds of our souls.

Brief biographies

Paul Lloyd is a ceramic artist, who was born and brought up in North Wales. A long-standing friend of the Pennant family, Paul is a native of Denbigh and now lives in St Asaph, a few miles from Tremeirchion. Just before it was sold, Paul volunteered to draw a sketch of Nantlys. In the end he went back to the house daily for many weeks doing sketches and pen and ink drawings of each elevation, and then drawings of every significant or eccentric room. He has good memories of playing croquet on summer afternoons on the big lawn at Nantlys.

Meyriel Edge grew up at The Salusbury Arms, next to the church and school, or, in her father's words, 'education, salvation, and damnation'. He said all three were necessary for a balanced life; she thought riding and drawing did the same thing.

She taught art at Mold's Alun School, Brynhyfryd in Ruthin, and St Brigidine's in Denbigh before moving to Charleston, South Carolina, where she continued to teach art for 24 more years. She now focuses on her own work and is also a very original milliner, enjoying the balance of 3D with her 2D work. Meyriel has completed 30 portraits of Tremeirchion people who were a treasured part of her upbringing. *Carriageworks* in Denbigh hosted a show of these portraits entitled *Salt of the Earth*. Many of the families mentioned in *On a Dark Night with Enough Wind...* were represented in the show.

S. Sinkow

Lilla Pennant grew up in Wales. She has worked as a freelance writer in London and New York. She has written two small books on remarkable civilian stories from both world wars. She has also worked in the field of family violence and published professional articles in this field. Lilla is working on a book about mystical experiences.